TRAVELLING MAN

A tribute to the
Life and Ministry of the
Reverend Dr Arthur Skevington Wood

Paul Taylor and Howard Mellor

Cliff College Publishing & The Wesley Fellowship

Scripture Quotations are taken from the Revised Authorized Version © 1982 Samuel Bagster & Sons Ltd and The Bible Societies.

ISBN 1 898362 05 X
Cliff College Publishing,
Cliff College, Calver,
Sheffield S30 1XG

ISBN 0 9516332 3 6
The Wesley Fellowship,
Stonebridge Cottage,
Back Lane, Shearsby,
Nr Lutterworth,
Leicestershire LE17 6PN

Typesetting, design and production oversight by:

MOORLEY'S Print & Publishing
23 Park Rd., Ilkeston, Derbys DE7 5DA
Tel/Fax: (0115) 932 0643

Printed at Redwood Books

CONTENTS

ERRATA

We regret that, due to repaging after the textual
proof corrections, the following were not changed:-

p.38	line 30	read	(see p.40)				
p.59	line 36	read	(see p.80):	p.80	read	(p.59)
p.64	line 24	read	(see p.80):	p.80	read	(p.64)
p.111	line 9	read	(see p.114):	p.114	read	(p.111)

Dr Wood at Paisley 1951 - 1957

FOREWORD

The many people who knew Dr Arthur Skevington Wood personally, as well as those who were greatly blessed and helped by his writings and preaching, will welcome this new biography. Dr Wood's life and ministry touched many people and its inspiration reached far beyond the Methodist Church of which he was a life-long member. In these pages readers will find information about Dr Wood's life not generally known which gives insight into his ministry and reflects something of the greatness of this gentle giant of a man - for spiritual giant he surely was. The biographical section, though concise, gives considerable detail about his background which readers will find both fascinating and informative. What clearly comes across is the massive contribution he made to Christ's Kingdom through the various aspects of his work: academic, literary, pastoral, educational and evangelistic. How well Dr Wood's life illustrated Dr James Denney's dictum: 'We need all our theologians to be evangelists and all our evangelists to be theologians.' Arthur Wood combined those often all-too-rare qualities in Church leaders and scholars: the informed head and the warmed heart. Never a sectarian or a bigot in any sense, he was nevertheless a shining example in his life and an enthusiastic promoter in his ministry of all that it means to be Wesleyan.

Because of Dr Wood's humble and self-effacing nature his achievements as scholar, writer and preacher have not been truly appreciated by the Church as a whole. This book helps to redress the balance and Paul Taylor must be warmly commended for researching the biographical section and his many other contributions to the biography. As this book is a joint venture between Cliff College and the Wesley Fellowship, it is appropriate that Dr Wood's contribution to both is detailed in some measure. But this represents only a small part of a very full, busy and dedicated life. It is difficult to express in words the gratitude owed to Dr Wood by all who knew him, whether members of his congregations, readers of his books, listeners to his sermons, staff colleagues or students. All will be glad that this biography has been written to honour the memory of Dr Arthur Skevington Wood.

William R. Davies
Herbert McGonigle

PREFACE

*'God weaves the pattern of our days according to his purpose
so that the glory may be His ....'*

A.S. Wood. 1993

General William Booth, conducting the dedication of his
granddaughter Catherine, began his address with these words, 'It
is a principle of the Salvation Army that everything we possess
belongs to God'. Arthur and Mary Wood did not have the gift of
grandchildren but they adopted the General's prescription for the
Christian way along every avenue of their lives. This book is
published to pay tribute to the life and varied ministry of a man
who received some of life's richest gifts and used them for the
glory of God.

Dr Arthur Skevington Wood was associated with Cliff College,
Sheffield, over a period of many years and was Principal for seven
of them. He helped to inaugurate and promote the Wesley
Fellowship and was President in its formative period up to his
death. His promotion to glory on 28th January 1993 presents an
opportunity for making available some aspects of his life and a
selection of his work.

In his book on Thomas Haweis, Dr Wood records the
sentiments of Haweis as he prepared to write the biography of
William Romaine. Haweis said in the Preface to the Romaine
biography that 'he hoped some better qualified author might have
appeared to do justice to the undertaking, with materials more
abundant, and capable of adorning his memory with trophies of
more excellent workmanship.' This modest publication by the
Wesley Fellowship and Cliff College cannot hope to do justice to
a man of many attributes and interests. It is hoped that others
with different resources will take up the challenge of writing a
full biography.

Meanwhile, what follows presents a cameo of a minister of the
gospel whose contribution to the evangelical cause involved
preaching, lecturing, writing and the pastoral ministry. To many
he was a mentor, to many more a friend and to all a Christian
gentleman who adorned the doctrines he believed.

The title *Travelling Man* calls for explanation. It is taken
from a lecture given by Dr Wood on the life of John Bunyan. It
seems appropriate to reflect the progress of the new life which
begins at conversion and continues into heaven. A traditional
Methodist description of its ministry is 'travelling' and the

world-wide itinerary of Dr Wood's work with the Movement for World Evangelisation, which occupied seven years of his middle life, involved extensive travel.

It is needful, as well as traditional, to express thanks for the help given in the writing of a book. It is our happy duty to thank all who have provided encouragement, time, skills, recollections and documents. A roll call of such valued helpers is given in Appendix II.

Above all, we wish to express our thanks to God for giving to us His servant, Arthur Skevington Wood, and for sustaining him in the exacting tasks of sanctified scholarship and biblical ministry.

> 'Leader of faithful souls, and guide
> Of all that travel to the sky,
> Come and with us, ev'n us abide,
> Who would on thee alone rely,
> On thee alone our spirits stay,
> While held in life's uneven way.'
>
> H & P 819   Charles Wesley

Our prayer in publishing this tribute to our friend is that the continuing influence of his work will enrich those who follow the example of his life and faith.

Paul Taylor, Lutterworth
Howard Mellor, Cliff College
October 1994

PART ONE

Arthur Skevington Wood

A Biographical Cameo

YEARS OF YOUTH

'Now thank we all our God, ...
Who, from our mothers' arms
Has blessed us on our way ....'

H & P 566   Martin Rinkart 1586-1649
                                       tr. Catherine Winkworth 1827-78

At the age of 11 years Arthur Skevington Wood made an important decision. From that time he would give his life to Jesus Christ. He writes: 'Two CSSM leaders got on to me after watching a hockey match and gave me no peace until I faced the challenge of the master!' CSSM had been engaged in an evangelistic mission in North Yorkshire and Arthur had met the team on the sands at Whitby. Little could they realise then what choice fruit was to result from that encounter.

Although the hand of God was upon the youthful disciple, it was not until five years later that he could testify to his evangelical conversion, facing the fact of sin in his life and accepting the pardon purchased at the Cross. This second and deeply felt experience occurred during a Methodist Group Fellowship house party and testimony was given to the work of grace during a communion service. This was one of the reasons why, throughout his life, the communion service was important to him.

From these early experiences of the love of God sprang the mainstream of Dr Skevington Wood's ministry. J. Ernest Rattenbury in his book *The Conversion of the Wesleys* (1938) writes of the critical experiences in the life of John Wesley. In 1725 Wesley, in an act of abandonment and dedication turned from worldliness to 'real religion.' Having read Thomas à Kempis and Jeremy Taylor, he decided on a completely religious life resolving that he would no longer be half a Christian but a real one. Although that 1725 decision was sincere, it made little difference to Wesley's spirituality or to the effectiveness of his work. The well recorded events of 1738 were of a different order. March 1738 found him in earnest conversations with the Moravian, Peter Bohler, on the question of saving faith. He began to realise the vital importance of justification by faith alone for personal salvation. At Whitsuntide in that memorable year the Spirit of God came upon him in an unusual way. His heart was strangely warmed, the experience of sins forgiven was felt through faith and the gift of assurance of salvation made it an 'epoch-making day.'

It may be suggested that the 'conversion' of 1725 was little more than a mental process and a human decision, whilst the 1738 crisis was the effectual working of God in the very soul of the man and so has been described as his 'evangelical conversion.' It certainly gave rise to the fervour and fire which marked all his future evangelistic work.

So, from two distinct but related events of great importance John Wesley and his 20th-century follower and spiritual son, Arthur Wood, launched their life's work of preaching and teaching the incomparable truths of scriptural Christianity.

Dr Skevington Wood, introducing John Wesley in his book *The Burning Heart* (1967) begins: 'With a shrewd flash of insight, John Wesley once told Adam Clarke: "If I were to write my own life I should begin before I was born."' The story of Arthur Wood can be traced back on the maternal side to Thomas and John Skevington, his great grandfather and great uncle. John Skevington (1815-45) was a Methodist Minister serving the cause of Christ in New Zealand. His death at a comparatively early age prevented him from seeing a breath of revival in the area of his ministry. Thomas Skevington (1827-1901) was involved in the Nottingham lace industry. Both men embraced wholeheartedly the ardour of earlier Methodism. The family of Thomas Skevington included four children, John, Emma, Charles and Mary Elizabeth (1853-1916). Mary Skevington's husband, John William Cooper (1854-98) was a craftsman in the building industry having a plumbing and glazing business in Alfreton Road, Nottingham.

Arthur's grandparents, John and Mary Cooper, were married on 25th July 1877 and their family included a daughter, May (1885-1970) who in her turn was to become the wife of a schoolteacher and local preacher, William Arthur Wood (1886-1964). Their only child, Arthur, was born in Ashbourne, Derbyshire, on 21st January 1916. So can be traced, in the providence of God, strands of Wesleyan revival, missionary vision, skilled workmanship, professional discipline and an educated mind in the son born to William and May Wood. All these richly inherited gifts would emerge in the later life and work of Arthur Skevington Wood.

It is not easy to discover many details of Arthur Wood's early life. As far as is known he was not a diarist in the John Wesley mould. The absence of other children in his family and his own childlessness contribute to the difficulty.

His parents moved from Ashbourne to Yarm in North Yorkshire, now Cleveland, when Arthur was an infant. This move was to enable William Wood to take up a teaching position at Yarm Grammar School and for many years he occupied the position of headmaster. Yarm Grammar School, despite a reputation for excellence in its academic and sporting activities, closed sometime in the 1970's and was opened again in 1978 as an independent fee-paying school.

Before entering his father's school Arthur had been educated privately and William and May Wood closely supervised his learning, encouraging him in the classics. He entered Yarm Grammar School at scholarship age and quickly showed his ability to learn with speed and accuracy. It was at school that Arthur began to love books and his two favourite places were the library and the sports field. He played both cricket and football to a standard better than average and maintained his interest in sport all his life, playing beyond school days and into college years. He explained on one occasion to his colleague at Cliff College, Revd Howard Belben, that he was chosen in football as a goalkeeper and at cricket as a wicket keeper, though he opened the batting too. Howard Belben's comment then was that both positions seemed to fit the role we saw him fulfil as an Apollos and Defender of the Faith. For those who know their sport, goalkeepers and wicket keepers have an important role, from their strategic positions in the field. They are encouragers. From where they play most of the vital action can be seen and they know where drooping heads need to be lifted up. Perhaps in this sporting analogy we can see the seeds of Dr Wood's ministry as a 20th-century Apollos and a Barnabas also.

It was in Yarm as a schoolboy that Arthur Wood was first introduced to Cliff College. Trekkers from the College visited the town. He began to realise the distinctive message and methods of the College at that early stage in his spiritual development. Many years later he could write: 'Although never a student at the College, I have always claimed to possess a Cliff heart. That is to say, my spirit coincides with the spirit of Cliff. I profoundly believe in its emphasis. For over thirty years ......I have proclaimed its message. Most important of all, I can testify to the experience of the cleansed heart and the infilling of the Spirit for which Cliff stands.'

The work of God in his young heart and the touch of God on his adolescent life were never hidden behind any of his later academic achievements or clouded by the development of his scholarly mind. All his work was marked by a happy blend of simplicity, clarity and spirituality which was the product of a deep experience of personal salvation.

At the end of his life when the travelling was all but over, Arthur Wood was in the hands of skilled physicians at the Royal Hallamshire Hospital, Sheffield. His testimony to his doctor, on hearing the prognosis of his last illness was: 'I am safe in the arms of Jesus.' The thanksgiving service for his life at Victoria Hall, Sheffield, included music chosen by Dr Wood as reflecting the reality and simplicity of his early Christian experience. The music was the familiar tune to the hymn 'From sinking sands he lifted me, with tender hands he lifted me, from shades of night to plains of light, O praise his Name, he lifted me.'

It seems entirely appropriate to encapsulate the early years of Dr Skevington Wood's life in Paul's biographical reference to Timothy ...... 'from childhood you have known the Holy Scriptures which are able to make you wise for salvation through faith which is in Christ Jesus.' 2 Tim. 3 v15 (RAV).

PREPARATION

'As for every man to whom God has given riches and wealth ...... to receive his heritage and rejoice in his labour - this is the gift of God. For he will not dwell unduly on the days of his life, because God keeps him busy with joy in his heart.'

Ecc. 5 vv 19-20 (RAV)

Arthur Wood entered Yarm Grammar School in 1927 and matriculated there in 1933. His experience of the converting power of the gospel at the age of 16 had caused him to ponder on the will of God for his life. What was it to be? The Lord had a plan for his life; of that he could be sure. As it gradually unfolded, it was to be a busy life and full of joy in the service of his Master. Here is a part of his testimony as he enters into a period of preparation for the fulfilment of God's will. 'It was the emptiness of life without Christ as I observed it in my contemporaries that drove me to become an evangelist. I believed then and still do that there is no more strategic position from which to win men and women to Christ than the local church.' Eventually he was to hear the call of God unmistakably to the full-time ministry of the church. That ministry with all its demands of biblical understanding, preaching, worship and pastoral care needed preparation. The confirmation of the call however, was to be delayed.

At the age of 18 it seemed right for Arthur to have more experience of life in the world of commerce. He entered the departmental store of Lewis's of Leeds to train for a managerial position. Such training has become sophisticated and intense in the latter years of our century, but it is not clear what was involved in those mid-thirties. We may be sure that some degree of administration and staff management would be included. Much more important was his shoulder-rubbing contacts with ambitious business executives and the people in the streets of Leeds.

At first it had seemed likely that a career in business beckoned, but it was not to be along that way he would travel for long. A sensitive Christian spirit began to see the needs around him which could not be met by any other means than through his Saviour, Jesus Christ. Even while still at school Arthur began to realise that there were intellectual reasons for believing the gospel. As God's hand was laid on Arthur's life at this time, he saw the ordained ministry in the Methodist Church as a platform from which he could reach out to those who needed both the life changing work of Jesus Christ and the mental equipment to deal with those inevitable questions raised both by a study of the bible and a response of faith which precedes the blessing of full salvation.

After two years of secular employment the seed of the call to the preaching and pastoral ministry began to bear its inevitable fruit, as Arthur Wood listened to the voice of God in his heart. Eventually, the call became so clear and insistent that it could no longer be put aside without disobedience. At the age of 20 he responded to the call, was accepted as a candidate for the Methodist ministry and in 1936 began his theological and pastoral preparations in Wesley College, Headingley, Leeds.

At his baptism his parents had prayed and expressed the desire that their son, to be their only child, would become a Christian and a preacher of the gospel. 'And let me live to preach thy word, and let me to Thy glory live.' Wesley's famous words and the aspirations of William and May Wood were to be fulfilled, probably even beyond their faith and hopes.

In the years when Arthur Wood was a student at Wesley College, Methodism and Headingley were particularly blessed with exceptional tutors. One such scholar was to be influential in Arthur Wood's college years. The Revd Dr Howard Watkin-Jones gently guided his student into historical studies. Later on in Arthur Wood's academic work he would find other men of outstanding ability and spirituality who would become his mentors. The Very Revd Dr Hugh Watt, Principal of New College, Edinburgh, was to suggest the subject of his doctorate, the result of which was the publication of his first book, *Thomas Haweis* (1957). He also came under the helpful influence of the Very Revd Dr Norman Sykes, sometime Dixie Professor of Ecclesiastical History at Cambridge, who maintained an interest in Dr Wood's work over many years.

During his training at Headingley Arthur studied theology and eventually graduated with a B.A. awarded by London University (1941). More important however, by the encouragement of Dr Watkin-Jones, he began to acquire the love of history which would eventually emerge as his main academic interest and which would result in the outstanding contributions he made to historical scholarship. He became deeply involved in the period of the 16th-Century Reformation and the evangelical revival in Britain in the 18th-Century. It was at Wesley College that he learned the skills of the biblical exegete and expositor which were to form the basis of all his preaching and teaching ministry, and much of his writing too. As the Apollos reference of Howard Belben implies, Arthur Wood was to become 'a learned man, with a thorough knowledge of the scriptures who had been instructed in the ways of the Lord, spoke with great fervour and taught about Jesus accurately' Acts 18 vv24-28 (RAV). Perhaps there can be no higher tribute to the evangelical integrity of Arthur Wood than to compare him with the stature of such a New Testament preacher.

The academic preparation was to be continued some six years later when he began to work on a doctoral thesis at New College, Edinburgh. His Director of Studies was the Revd John H.S. Burleigh, who encouraged and supervised the research undertaken on the significant but relatively unknown Anglican evangelical, Thomas Haweis (1734-1820), Rector of Aldwincle in Northamptonshire. This study allowed Arthur Wood to examine the fascinating relationship between the Wesleyan revival and the parallel movement in Anglicanism led by Henry Venn, William Romaine, Charles Simeon and others.

The Apostle Paul, writing to Timothy, his young protégé and son in the faith said '... I was appointed a preacher, an apostle and a teacher ...' 2 Tim.1 v11 (RAV). So too was Arthur Skevington Wood and his preparation for this high calling had been marked by thoroughness, discipline and joy.

Dr Carl Henry with Arthur and Mary Wood at Cliff College

STATIONS

'His adorable will
Let us gladly fulfil
And our talents improve
By the patience of hope and the labour of love!'
H & P 354   Charles Wesley

In a letter to his friend Mr Storie, Oliver Cromwell wrote:
'Amongst the catalogue of those good works which your fellow
citizens and countrymen have done, this will not be reckoned for
the least; that they have provided for the feeding of the souls.'
Not the least that may be said of Dr Skevington Wood's ministry
is that he was a careful shepherd, feeding his people with the
choicest of food and serving both his Master and his people with
love and loyalty. His circuit ministry in the Methodist Church
was to extend over twenty-two years.

The Revd Arthur Skevington Wood was first stationed by
Conference in 1940 to the Glasgow Parkhead and Burnbank
Circuit, and he was to spend three profitable years in Scotland's
largest city and near to the scenes of the great Cambuslang
revival of 1742. It was here, in his first circuit work, that Dr
Wood's preaching developed into a thoroughly evangelical
presentation of the gospel based on biblical exposition. It has
been said that Arthur Wood's preaching 'bore the stamp of the
finest Scottish tradition. His sermons were expository and
theological, clear in outline and language and prepared with
meticulous attention to detail.'

Towards the end of his first Scottish pastorate, Arthur was
married, at the earliest opportunity allowed by Methodist rules,
on 1st January 1943. A new year and a new life began on that
special day. His bride, Mary Fearnley, was born in 1913 at Leigh
in Lancashire. She was converted to Christ as a teenager and
quickly became active in church and Sunday School work. She
and Arthur had met four years earlier at a Christian Endeavour
Holiday Home where her husband-to-be was an excursion leader.
Mary was to become a tower of strength, a true partner in all Dr
Wood's work and a model minister's wife for over 50 years. The
Revd Howard Belben writes: 'Service as a local missionary
secretary led to a sense of call to overseas service, but her
mother's health prevented any immediate response.' There was,
happily, to be a partial fulfilment of that calling as Mary

accompanied her husband on his later foreign travels and at Cliff College where she was able to take more than a usual interest in students arriving from other countries and cultures.

In the leading of God, Arthur Wood was not to remain in Scotland and he travelled south to the English Midlands, to the Brierley Hill circuit and to Stourbridge, where he was to spend three years of further pastoral work and preaching. It was during this period, in fact in 1945, that Arthur Wood's interest in local preachers and their training was first officially recognised by his appointment to the Connexional Committee for local preachers. He remained a valuable member of that Committee for six years until he took responsibility for the Paisley Central Hall.

Scotland was again to be the scene of his developing work as he was inducted into the Coatbridge and Airdrie circuit on the east side of Glasgow. He remained in this large circuit for five years, during which time he began his association with New College, Edinburgh, and its Dean, the Very Revd Hugh Watts. This association eventually culminated in the award of the Doctor of Philosophy degree to which reference has already been made.

September 1951 saw Dr Wood move to the west of Glasgow, to Paisley Central Hall. At Paisley he had ministerial oversight of what was probably one of the largest Methodist congregations in Scotland and he responded typically with dependence on God. It was a demanding task to lead a great Central Hall in all its many and varied aspects of Christian service to the community. Although Dr Wood was always a diligent and compassionate pastor, his preaching was, for him, an important part of his ministry. Professor I. Howard Marshall of Aberdeen writes: 'Arthur Skevington Wood first came to my notice in my student days when he was the speaker at the annual rally in our Methodist circuit. I accompanied my father to hear him with somewhat mixed expectations. I hadn't heard many good Methodist preachers up to that point in my life. A young man, resplendent in the Ph.D. hood of Edinburgh University, announced his text. "But God forbid that I should glory except in the cross of our Lord Jesus Christ, by whom the world has been crucified to me, and I to the world," Gal. 6v14 (RAV), and then preached the gospel with extraordinary effectiveness.'

Arthur and Mary Wood were welcomed into the life of the Paisley Central Hall on Sunday, 2nd September 1951 following a mid-century evangelistic campaign involving most denominations in Paisley. As soon as he arrived, Dr Wood was instrumental in forming the Ministers' Fraternal, and became involved in the Paisley Council of Churches, taking part in open air meetings and children's work.

The Superintendent's message for the 1952 anniversary captures Dr Wood's enthusiastic commitment to evangelism. He wrote: 'Every part of our church has given its mind to this important matter,' referring to the coming crusade in the following year. 'We seek to be a people prepared for the Lord in the year of advance' he wrote, and continued: 'We are persuaded that one of the most effective ways of being ready for evangelism in 1953 is to be engaged in it already.'

A Cliff College delegation led by the incomparable Tom Butler held a two week campaign in February 1952, which resulted in seven members accepting the call to preach and one hearing the call to the Methodist ministry. A Cliff Fellowship was formed which was to last actively for several years. As could be expected, the Superintendent encouraged the fellowship, which numbered up to 50 with ages ranging between 14 and 50.

The year 1954 was hectic for the minister and people of Paisley Mission. The theme for the year was 'Building on the results of the year of evangelism.' Dr Wood writes in the anniversary brochure: 'During and since the year of evangelism, 67 new members have been received into the church ... after regular attendance at preparation class,' and again, '11 adult baptisms have taken place before a worshipping congregation and in themselves have been an impressive witness to the gospel.' Prayer was never neglected. Dr Wood goes on: 'Our weekly prayer meeting has grown in numbers and power and the League of Prayer, which binds its members in a daily fellowship, has also increased.'

The All Scotland Crusade of 1955, led by Dr Billy Graham, found Arthur Wood immersed in preparation, participation and follow-up. Fired with the enthusiasm of the Cliff Fellowship, many others, both members and non-members of the Central Hall, were caught up in the great events of the crusade. The Revd Tom Allen wrote: 'Dr Skevington Wood, the distinguished minister of the Methodist Central Hall in Paisley, was a member of the Counselling and Follow-up Committee and co-chairman of the Designating Committee.'

It was in 1955 also that Dr Wood was involved in a Methodist pulpit exchange with the Revd Wilbur G. Grose, of Simpson Church, Minneapolis, Minnesota. During his stay in the United States, Dr Wood undertook a full schedule of preaching, speaking and lecturing appointments at churches, luncheon clubs, colleges, conventions, camps and youth clubs, as well as appearing on radio and television broadcasts. Best of all, he had the joy of seeing souls won for Christ in response to the preaching of the gospel.

On his return, however, Dr Wood made some perceptive comments on American Christianity and American Methodism. They appeared in the Quarterly Newsletter of the Methodist Revival Fellowship. He had expected to find a form of godliness, even if the power was lacking, but even the form was not substantial. He was concerned about the attitude to the Lord's day. Morning worship and then pleasure was the order of the day. He writes: 'This virtual bisection of the Lord's day is perhaps the most saddening feature of American Methodism;' although it was some relief to him to learn that Methodist leaders were also deeply anxious. 'Methodism, on each side of the Atlantic, stands in need of Pentecostal revival,' he writes. Dr Wood's other concerns were the emphasis he found on the social gospel so-called, and the widespread lack of Methodist fervour. He did, however, find one or two Methodist churches on his travels where there was a faithfulness, a full schedule of worship and fellowship, attendance at weekly prayer meetings and a declaration of the gospel of full salvation. In this at least he could rejoice.

Tom Allen was to lead the Tell Scotland Campaign in 1956, and again, not surprisingly the Paisley Superintendent led and vigorously encouraged his people in participation. He wrote to them: 'The church can only be one hundred per cent effective when the congregation is one hundred per cent sanctified,' and later he is able to write: 'In the period of my own ministry here we have had the joy of receiving five fully accredited local preachers onto the circuit plan, we have five more at present on trial ... one candidate for the ministry has already completed his training and another is being presented this year.'

There are still seven members of Paisley Methodist Mission who recall the ministry of Dr Wood with great appreciation. They write: 'Perhaps one of the aspects of Dr Wood's ministry which meant so much to us was his Bible studies. On Sunday evenings throughout the winter, at Cliff Fellowship meetings, Dr Wood could be found (knees and toes together to form a lap for his open Bible) expounding the scriptures.'

His interest in the varied life of Paisley Central Hall extended to the Boys' Brigade. On arriving at Paisley, Dr Wood admitted that he knew little of the uniformed organisations. He soon learned to appreciate the opportunities and potential of the Boys' and Girls' Brigades, and he retained an affection for, and an interest in them, all his life. He became Chaplain to the brigades at Paisley and it was a joy to him to see as many as 170 young people on parade at anniversary services. An even greater joy was to have the privilege of influencing their lives for Jesus Christ, when he spoke to them as a group several times a year.

The last two ministerial appointments for Dr Wood were in England. The Conference stationed him at Sunderland for the years 1957 to 1959 and it was during this time that he wrote and published his second book *And with Fire* (1958). The book was a series of addresses on the subject of revival, a matter which was to become a key factor in his life and work. His desire and prayer to the end of his life was that God would be pleased to visit this land again in revival power. That he was to be disappointed in this hope was surely no reflection on his own total commitment to prayer and evangelism.

His passion for revival was expressed in his early membership and support of the Methodist Revival Fellowship founded in 1948. The early pioneers of this movement, with its emphasis on prayer for revival, had an able and enthusiastic ally in Dr Skevington Wood. He was to play an active role in the MRF over many years, speaking at numerous prayer conferences held annually at Swanwick. His support was extended when the movement Conservative Evangelicals In Methodism (CEIM) was begun in order to emphasise the theological implications of prayer, evangelism and revival from a conservative evangelical standpoint. He was an active member of Headway, which eventually took over the twin roles of MRF and CEIM. Dr Wood wrote and spoke for all these organisations in Methodism and, using Paul's words, he had them in his heart.

His final circuit appointment was to York Wesley and to the Southlands Church, during which period another important book was to be written. 1960 saw the publication of what was, some believe, his finest work, *The Inextinguishable Blaze*, a review of the events of the 18th-Century revival on which he was to become an international authority. *The Inextinguishable Blaze* appeared as Volume 6 of a series on the advance of Christianity through the centuries edited by Professor F.F. Bruce. 'A thrilling story of the 18th-century awakenings with a blend of accurate scholarship and evangelical understanding' (Dr G.W. Bromiley).

In the last year of his circuit ministry, Dr Wood was invited to contribute to the IVP *New Bible Dictionary* and that valuable reference book contains several articles by him.

Billy Graham returned to England for the North of England Crusade in Manchester in 1961 whilst Dr Wood was at York, and this gave him a further opportunity to support what had become a deep commitment to the task of evangelism on a large and orderly scale.

In 1949 during his Coatbridge and Airdrie ministry, Dr Wood began a long association with the *Evangelical Quarterly*, at the time when the Editor was his Edinburgh University Director of Studies, Professor John Burleigh. In over 40 years of involvement with the Evangelical Quarterly Dr Wood contributed nearly 100 articles and book reviews. The index of his contributions includes John Newton's Church History; Luther Today; Nicholas of Lyra; Luther's Concept of Revelation; Social Involvement in the Apostolic Church; Luther as a Preacher and the Eschatology of Irenaeus. He was also asked to write the tribute to another distinguished Editor, Professor F.F. Bruce, on his retirement in 1981. Of Dr Wood's contribution to the E.Q., Professor Howard Marshall writes: 'He remained active almost to the end despite ill health. His last review was dated 29th December 1992, and it was accompanied by a note apologising for his untidy typescript due to the effects of Parkinson's disease ... He was a discerning reviewer and a wise counsellor, and above all a source of encouragement and inspiration to me personally in his remarkable combination of a faithful and effective preacher of the gospel and a meticulous scholar of the highest calibre.'

The extraordinarily wide interests of Dr Wood can be appreciated from the organisations in which he was involved. At various times he was Vice President of the National Young Life Campaign, the Evangelistic Society, the Lord's Day Observance Society, and in 1959 he was elected President of the Christian Endeavour Union. If that was not enough, he was also for some time the Chairman of the Research Group at Tyndale House, Cambridge, and because of his valued contributions to the Wesley Historical Society he became a life member of that organisation. His scholarship in the field of church history resulted in his election to the Fellowship of the Royal Historical Society, an honour received only by nomination.

How could a man combine successfully so many demanding aspects of work? It could only be by a discipline of time and a conservation of energy for the primary tasks of service. In the

secret place of the heart burned the fire of love for the Saviour.
God, in Christ, had given so much - so much should be returned.

> 'My Saviour, how shall I proclaim,
> How pay the mighty debt I owe?
> Let all I have, and all I am,
> Ceaseless to all thy glory show.'

H & P 743
                                              Paul Gerhardt (1607-76)
                                              tr. John Wesley 1703-91)

*Cliff team (Left to right): Revd John Job, Revd Brian Hoare,
Revd Dr Arthur Skevington Wood and Mr Ronald Abbott*

Two Cliff College Principals, Revd Howard Belben and Dr Wood

WIDENING WAYS

'Now the word doth swiftly run,
Now it wins its widening way,'
H & P 781   Charles Wesley

The gospel has widened its influence from the days of Jesus
and the apostles in Jerusalem, to the limits of the world.
Evangelists and messengers of the gospel, have taken its truth as
they have travelled over land and sea to nations near and far.

Dr Skevington Wood was an evangelist, a man with an
apostolic zeal for the winning of souls. He was a preacher of
fundamentals, not superficialities. His appeal was to both mind
and heart. His desire was that his hearers should know the truth
and that through the truth they should be free. He was now to
embark on a phase of his journey which would enable him to take
the word of God throughout the world.

Professor Howard Marshall has written about Dr Wood's gift
for evangelism. He says: 'Recently Dr David Hubbard, the
retiring President of the Fuller Seminary, commented that we
should not think of ourselves as scholars who happen to be
disciples, but as disciples who happen to be scholars. Arthur
Wood was an evangelist who happened to be a scholar.' C.S.
Lewis commented: 'We need two sorts of evangelists; evangelists
for the head and evangelists for the heart.' Better still surely, we
need evangelists who can satisfy both the questionings of the
mind and the aspirations of the heart. Dr Wood, in all his long
and fruitful ministry in circuit, as a travelling preacher, college
tutor and prolific writer was essentially an evangelist in it all.
He could speak eloquently to the intellect and the emotions. He
knew, as Wesley did, that an intellectual assent to the truths
about Jesus Christ was inadequate for salvation. What was also
needed was a personal trust in Christ as a Saviour sufficient to
satisfy the righteous demands of God and the deepest needs of
the human heart. He would echo Charles Wesley: 'What we have
felt and seen with confidence we tell.' Dr Wood wrote: 'Wesley
countered the current wave of rationalistic scepticism with a
ringing re-affirmation of those fundamental and supernatural
realities of the gospel which, whilst by no means incompatible
with reason, nevertheless transcend and surpass it.' *The Burning
Heart* (1967 p.15).

Revival was for Arthur Wood linked inextricably with prayer and evangelism. He had been taking part in discussions as a member of a Methodist team, forming a working party with Anglicans, on the theology of mission. He commented afterwards to Peter Barker of Headway: 'If we had spent all this time on evangelism and prayer for revival we would have made more progress in the kingdom of God.'

All of this is why Arthur Wood came eagerly and willingly into the arena of the great evangelistic campaigns of the post-war period. He hoped and prayed that the effectiveness of the large crusades in England and Scotland might lead to a deeper spiritual awakening in the land. Scenes in the Tell Scotland Crusade and in the missions of Billy Graham of men and women turning to Christ thrilled his heart. Wembley in 1955, Manchester in 1961, Earls Court in 1966 and 1967, seven major centres of population in 1984 and 1985 and London in 1989 all resulted in converts on an unprecedented scale. Arthur Wood saw this as an answer to prayer and a result of effective gospel preaching. Yet he longed for more. He tells of a conversation on one of his visits to America in 1958: 'My companion was Dr Paul S. Rees ... associate of Billy Graham ... and over a memorable meal table we were discussing what God had wrought through the All Scotland Crusade ... in which we had both been implicated. One question burned in each of our hearts, it was this - was revival about to break out in the land of the lochs and set the heather ablaze for Jesus Christ? We agreed that it would be unwise yet to speak of revival. Strong evangelism there certainly was but the "Divine disorder," as Thomas Chalmers used to term it ... had not yet manifested itself on any widespread scale ...' *And with Fire* (1958. p.5). The delay in the coming of revival only served to sharpen his focus on evangelism and his gifted role of encouraging by example the teaching of the truths of the New Testament.

The year 1962 brought a change of direction to the lives of Arthur and Mary Wood. They were released by Conference to join the Movement for World Evangelisation and to engage in a world-wide travelling ministry of preaching and teaching. Instead of a settled local church-based work in a Methodist circuit, the world was to be his circuit.

The Movement for World Evangelisation had begun in the years between the two world wars. Dr Thomas Cochrane, a missionary strategist, had become concerned to bring some unity of purpose and method to a variety of missionary societies and the means which were employed. A new magazine *World Dominion* was published as a means of assessing and evaluating different ways of bringing the message of the gospel to peoples of varied cultures. M.W.E. was concerned, in those years, with an examination of missionary trends and engaged in research projects to co-ordinate missionary strategies. The work in the post-war period became focused in Britain at the Filey Christian Holiday Crusade under the inspiring leadership of A. Lindsay Glegg. The Filey week attracted speakers from the U.S.A., including Dr Paul Rees, and the need now was to recruit more preachers and teachers. Dr Wood joined the staff in that capacity. Although there was a general oversight given by the M.W.E. leadership, all members of the staff were responsible for arranging their own itinerary and speaking arrangements. It was during his work with M.W.E. that Dr Wood extended his convention and conference ministry, travelling throughout Britain and to parts of Africa, Australia, Europe, the Caribbean, the Middle East, U.S.A., India, Taiwan, South Korea and the Philippines. During these visits there were opportunities to meet Christian leaders of the world-wide church, and he became acquainted with many well know Christians like Gladys Aylward and Mother Teresa. He spoke of his friendships with them with affection and humility.

The demands on Dr Wood as a convention and conference speaker is illustrated by Dr Frederick Tatford in the introduction to *For All Seasons* (1979), a collection of some of Arthur Wood's sermons. He writes: 'At a meeting to select a speaker for an important convention various names had been suggested and rejected, when one member impatiently asked what sort of man was required. This crystallised the whole matter. It must be someone of attractive personality, capable of delivering a series of scholarly addresses which should not be deadly dull, but of such a freshness and vitality as to appeal and inspire. There was only one answer and, as on many other occasions, there was unanimous agreement that the man needed was Arthur Skevington Wood. As a preacher and teacher Dr Wood is unequalled for his matter and clarity, and it is not surprising that he has a wide appeal.'

Dr Wood took an active interest in all that was afoot as conversations took place between Methodists and Anglicans about church union. His stance was a carefully considered opposition to the union proposals. He believed that a scrutiny of scripture revealed discrepancies between the nature of the New Testament church and the proposed amalgamated church. There were disastrous consequences, he believed, in allowing the pure truth of God to be sullied by the opinions of men on the three vital subjects of the priesthood, episcopacy and sacraments. His position was made clear in an article he wrote on the conversations for the Methodist Revival Fellowship entitled 'The Conversations and the Word of God'. Although the whole issue of organised union has receded somewhat at the present time, the issues which concerned those who opposed union then are still relevant today, as the church of Christ, for the most part, drifts into deeper confusion about the essential elements of scriptural and historic Christianity.

Dr Wood's first visit as a speaker to the Keswick Convention was in 1962. Methodist preachers have not occupied the platform at Keswick as often as those from other denominations, but Arthur Wood was to be a regular speaker and revisited Keswick on three other occasions until 1976, when by that time he was about to embark on the demanding principalship of Cliff College. One more visit to the Convention at Keswick was in 1992, the year that his wife Mary died. The Convention Council generously invited Dr Wood to attend as a member of the speakers' party to act as pastoral adviser and to conduct the epilogue. Dr Wood regarded this as a singular honour and privilege and said that it had been the happiest of weeks for him; he had been in his natural element. Arthur Wood had also become a familiar and respected figure at other conventions, regularly visiting the M.W.E. Filey convention and the Southport Methodist holiness convention, which had strong links with Cliff College.

Despite a heavy programme of speaking and travelling Dr Wood had not neglected his writing. This period of his life saw the publication of important contributions to the evangelical book scene. *Paul's Pentecost* appeared in 1963, being a study of Romans Chapter 8 and the person and work of the Holy Spirit in the life of the Christian. This was followed in the same year by *Heralds of the Gospel*, Dr Wood's treatise on preaching, dealing with the message, the method and the motive for preaching. The book *Prophecy in a Space Age* (1964) saw the author embark on, for him, an unfamiliar subject, science and the Bible. He believed and maintained that however far scientific discovery reached, it would never take man beyond his fundamental need of a personal knowledge of God. He then returned to more familiar subjects, *Evangelism*, a study in the theology and practice of evangelism appeared in 1966, and in 1967 *Principles of Biblical*

Interpretation was written and published. This book developed out of the author's concern to help students to find their way through the maze of theories of biblical interpretation. The same year saw the publication of one of Dr Wood's most important works, *The Burning Heart*, a full-scale biography of John Wesley as an evangelist and an examination of Wesley's ministry of evangelism. Although dealing with an 18th Century scene, it is relevant today. Dr Wood suggested that knowing what made John Wesley a soul-winning witness in his day can do much to make soul-winners in our day too. The Revd Dr Herbert McGonigle believes this book to be among the best four or five books ever written on John Wesley. Its popularity was such that it remained in print until 1992.

Dr Skevington Wood's interest in Martin Luther and the 16th Century Reformation period of Church History had begun in college years. It was in 1969 after many years of study and research that *Captive to the Word* was published. Subtitled 'Martin Luther, Doctor of Sacred Scripture', the book is a record of Luther's great passion for the word of God and a historical and theological appraisal of the Reformation perspective.

Thankfully, God has given a variety of gifts to this church. Dr Wood was himself such a gift. The 'Spirit gifts' and their purpose, as Paul refers to them in his Epistle to the Ephesians, were perfectly descriptive of Dr Wood's service to the church of Christ.

' ... And He himself gave some to be ... evangelists and some pastors and teachers, for the equipping of the saints for the work of ministry, for the edifying of the body of Christ till we all come to the unity of the faith and the knowledge of the Son of God, to a perfect man, to the measure of the stature of the fullness of Christ ... ' Ephesians 4 vv11-13 (RAV).

CLIFF COLLEGE
By John Job

'Many are called but few are choice' Samuel Chadwick

Appointments to Cliff and indeed to other Methodist positions of responsibility were made in a much less formal way a quarter of a century ago compared with contemporary rigour in such matters. No doubt the fundamental reason why Arthur Skevington Wood became the tutor in church history and Christian doctrine was that the Principal, Howard Belben, saw in him a person who would admirably fill the bill. At an earlier stage, Arthur Wood had wished to apply for a teaching post outside Methodism, but had loyally acceded to the refusal which then greeted his application. In the years immediately before his appointment at the college, he had (this time with Conference approval) been working for the Movement for World Evangelism. Certainly he was no mean speaker where evangelism was concerned. But his great gift of lucid historical writing meant that he was in his element in the kind of environment which Cliff provided. There was ample scope for preaching expeditions. There was reasonable time for research and writing. He was an excellent teacher with very clear presentation in everything he set his hand to, and he had a warm pastoral heart when it came to the students' multifarious problems.

The evangelical movement with which Cliff has always been associated is one which has tended to distance itself from the Methodist Church in which the college originated. This was partly because of theological differences with roots going back to the liberalism which characterised Methodism. At an earlier stage there had been an anti-intellectualism at Cliff which contrasted sharply with the climate of excessive regard for education prevalent in the church. There were also sociological factors which made it hard for Cliff to fit into its life. Tom Meadley had his struggle with a mixture of these problems, and Howard Belben addressed them too. But it was the historian in Arthur which enabled him to recognise most clearly what they amounted to and in various ways he saw his principalship as an opportunity for mending fences with Methodism.

The fact that the Peak circuit had to reduce staff just at the moment when he and Mary moved into Cliff House opened the door straightaway to a much closer relationship with local

Methodists. The invitation came for one of the Cliff tutors to take pastoral charge of a nearby chapel. At the same time closer links were made between the college and the chapel at Calver itself. The result was a greater warmth in the relationship between the college and the circuit than had previously been the case.

The intellectual range of students coming to Cliff was wider than that of the British army. Some of them had good results at A level. One or two could scarcely read and write. In between was a mixture of all shades of ability. The commonest situation was that of men and women in their early twenties who had not been motivated in their teens to make the most of their educational opportunities. Now they had become Christians and were looking to their year at Cliff for the chance to make up this lost ground. Arthur had the gifts necessary to cater for this wide range of students. Some went on to get first class degrees and doctorates; but he was concerned for lame dogs who had to be helped over stiles as well.

He had a particular interest in encouraging suitable men and women to offer for the ministry. Opportunities for lay pastors emerged in much greater number during the late seventies and eighties, and while few were in a position to go straight to a ministerial training college from Cliff, it became more and more important to find the right appointment to act as a bridge as well as an effective test of their call. Arthur had great skill both at discerning those who had the right gifts, and also at matching appointments to those concerned.

It is sometimes said that the inhabitants of Cliff are more varied than Noah's ark and the college gets more than its ration of extroverts each year. When this 'verray parfit gentil knyght', (see p. 33.) as he was called at Synod when he was retiring, succeeded as Principal, it was a question in many minds whether he would find some of the students hard to cope with, and whether discipline might become a problem. Such misgivings could hardly have been further from the mark. Arthur and Mary used to have almost all their meals in the dining room, and this straightaway had a dramatic effect on the degree of civilisation experienced there. But it was symbolic of a determination to be the father and mother of a family, which otherwise, of course, they never had. During the time that he was Principal there was remarkably little trouble. He expected respect. He earned it. And he received it from the roughest of diamonds, no doubt because there was no aloofness about his academic stature or what can only be called his saintliness.

This shone forth particularly at the class meeting, which was then held every Tuesday night. He used to read his sermons. But more than most men who do so, he maintained the interest of his congregation: and his material was unfailingly of a very high quality and was regarded as a tonic as much by his colleagues as by his students. Perhaps there was something old-fashioned about the structure and style of his addresses. But he had a keen sense of humour which lit up his illustrations and, impossible to miss, an insistent spirituality as he applied the message of his text.

After he became Principal he did not generally go out on missions with the students, as otherwise the tutors did, and as, more often than not, his predecessor had. He had not quite the same capacity for leading from the front, and the problem otherwise for a tutor is to avoid being or feeling something of a spare part. The Easter mission often required of the tutor to be a banker of sorts, with the task of working out claims for travel and expenses. This was not his scene at all, and it was amusing that he used to have Frank Blackwell, who had preceded Jack Henderson as the Administrative Officer, to come from Cliff to wherever the mission might be (often a hundred miles away) to keep his accounts straight.

Dr Wood's writing continued unabated during his period at Cliff. A number of books appeared including *Signs of the Times* (1970), a study of the prophetic signs leading up to the second coming of Christ. *The Nature of Man* (1972) was one of a series of books published by Scripture Union under the general title of *Understanding Bible Teaching*. *For All Seasons* (1979) was a selection of Dr Wood's sermons published to allow a wider public to have access to his preaching, and *I Want To know What The Bible Says About God* (1980) was issued by Kingsway in a series edited by Revd Gilbert Kirby.

Latterly he was not a fit man. He had a hernia which he only had dealt with after he retired. Both he and Mary had problems with blood pressure, though they did not give the impression that they found their exacting work stressful. And then a year or two before he left, he was very seriously ill with an attack of pneumonia which looked at one stage as if it would prove fatal. In the event, he made a fair recovery, although his voice was never again to have the same timbre. He had somehow contrived to fit his illness into the summer holidays, so he was ready for the autumn term when it began. When it came to the question of his re-appointment, he was ready to undertake a further three years. But the committee, reckoning that this would bring him nearly to his seventieth birthday, and that there had been an undoubted sapping of vitality which could not be expected fully to return, decided that this would be an unwise undertaking.

The year of his retirement, 1983, was also the centenary of the college. He often laughed at the joke when he said that Cliff was the only college which started as a newspaper: Joyful News led to the decision on Thomas Champness's part to train men in the wake of its success for lay ministry and evangelism. The event in February of that year was celebrated in style: the great Cliff Hall was heated for the wintry occasion by two enormous convectors at either end, looking for all the world like jet engines under testing! For one who was so well versed in, and enthusiastic about, the history of the college - as indeed about the Reformation, the Evangelical Revival and every other aspect of church history - this was a very fitting finale to his six years as Principal.

He was already past sixty when he took on the task, and was perhaps seen by some as a caretaker paving the way for one or other of a wider selection of candidates a few years later. In retrospect this would be a gross underestimate of his achievement. Interestingly, while many of the Principals at Cliff have marked their tenure of the post by some addition to the buildings, Arthur Wood in his comparable contribution established a much better basis for the evangelistic staff, remarking with quiet satisfaction that extending the ministry of the college was more appropriate for those who believed that here we have no abiding city.

REFERENCE

Chaucer, *Canterbury Tales, Prologue* 1.72

RESIDUE OF DAYS

'Sing to the great Jehovah's praise;
All praise to him belongs;
Who kindly lengthens out our days
Demands our choicest songs.

Our residue of days or hours
Thine, wholly thine, shall be,
And all our consecrated powers
A sacrifice to thee.'
H & P 360   Charles Wesley

Following the demands of Cliff College with its wide range of responsibilities it would have been entirely reasonable if Dr Wood was to wind down and enjoy his retirement. But this was not in his nature. Retirement was but to enter into a new phase of work, albeit perhaps without the vigour of earlier years.

Arthur and Mary Wood chose to live in Sheffield. A bungalow in Beauchief, an attractive southern suburb of the city, was made available to them. Sheffield enabled them to live reasonably near to Cliff College and it was central for what travelling they were still to do. More importantly it allowed him to join and take part in the activities of Victoria Hall Methodist Church and renew his love for Central Hall mission work.

The Victoria Hall minister, the Revd Allan Hughes, has paid tribute to the part played by Dr Wood in the life and work of the mission. Despite Dr Wood's reputation as a scholar and preacher, for him to sit in the congregation with his eagerness to participate made preaching easier rather than harder. Though he was by temperament a traditionalist, he could take part in the more modern expressions of worship without losing his enjoyment or his characteristic smile.

Unfortunately both Arthur and Mary Wood suffered a growing degree of debilitating illness both before and during the years of retirement. Mary had to learn how to live with a heart condition from the early seventies. Arthur himself was diabetic, but most serious of all, 1986 saw the onset of Parkinson's disease which was to hinder him increasingly in his remaining years. Indifferent health was to become a handicap, but it was never allowed to be a burden and the output of work was not seriously affected until 1991, a year or so before his death.

Two further important books were to come from his pen, *The Call of God* published by the Overseas Missionary Fellowship in 1984 and *Revelation and Reason* published by the Wesley Fellowship in 1992 and dedicated to the memory of his wife, Mary. The Inter-Varsity Press published its new *Dictionary of Theology* in 1988 and Dr Wood contributed several articles to that volume. He remained committed to preparing reviews and articles for the *Evangelical Quarterly*, the *Epworth Review*, the *Wesley Historical Society Proceedings* and numerous other papers and journals.

Dr Wood was still in demand both as a preacher and conference speaker and he travelled widely during these supposedly easier years.

Although a substantial part of his library remained at Cliff College he was nevertheless proud to show his frequent visitors that part of it which crowded, with orderly compactness, his small bungalow home. He did not leave behind his orderly life either. Each day, right up to 1992, saw him at his desk, with his new typewriter, for several hours each day, working in 'shifts' with a break of an hour or so in between.

His reputation as a biblical scholar of international repute had been established during the earlier part of his life, but the invitation to deliver the Drew Lecture on 'Immortality' in 1963 was a recognition of the esteem in which he was held. He had contributed articles to the *New International Dictionary of the Christian Church*, produced by Paternoster in 1974, and had written the commentary on the Epistle to the Ephesians for the *Expositors' Bible Commentary* issued by Zondervan in 1978. This last work enabled him to express his gift for lucid and relevant exposition of scripture. The *Expositors' Bible Commentary* edited by Frank E. Gaebelein was described as 'written primarily by expositors for expositors.'

One feature of Dr Wood's retirement years which gave him pleasure was his association with the Wesley Fellowship. For some years the Revd Dr Herbert McGonigle, Principal of the Nazarene Theological College in Manchester had noted, with appreciation, the service rendered by the Westminster Fellowship to its members. Largely due to the inspiration and leadership of its founder, Dr Martin Lloyd Jones, it arranged gatherings in London and elsewhere and published papers, dealing mainly with the historical, biblical and theological aspects of the Reformed faith. A need was felt for a similar fellowship which would bring together those who were enthusiastic about a Wesleyan understanding of the Christian faith. A number of ministers eventually agreed that such a fellowship would be desirable. In 1984 progress was made when Herbert McGonigle and the Revd Dr William Parkes, a Methodist minister in Staffordshire, were found to share the same enthusiasm for a Wesleyan fellowship. After a number of informal discussions a further meeting was held in the Tunstall Methodist Church, Stoke-on-Trent, on 22nd February 1985. About 35 people attended and it was agreed to launch a Wesleyan fellowship. The inaugural meeting was planned for September 1985. A discussion took place about who should be invited to present the first Occasional Paper and the Revd Dr Arthur Skevington Wood was chosen. He was a scholar of international standing, fully Wesleyan in persuasion and, in particular, committed to Wesley's teaching on scriptural holiness. He readily agreed to present a paper and, to facilitate his attendance, the meeting was held in the Highfield Methodist Church, London Road, Sheffield, on 21st September 1985. Dr Wood delivered a carefully prepared lecture, subsequently published as *Love Excluding Sin*.

A number of names had been proposed for the newly formed fellowship, and it was eventually agreed that the name should be The Wesley Fellowship. This was formally adopted in 1986. By common agreement, Dr McGonigle was appointed Chairman, Dr Parkes, Secretary and Treasurer, and by unanimous choice Dr Skevington Wood became the first President, continuing in that office until his death in 1993. Because of ill health and other commitments he was not able to attend every biannual meeting, but his interest and encouragement was always enthusiastic. He did attend meetings in 1992 and was preparing to give the 1993 Annual Lecture on William Bramwell when serious ill health intervened.

During this last decade of varied experiences, the bitter-sweet order of life brought opportunities for Arthur and Mary to express their capacity for friendships. New friends were made at Victoria Hall, some of whom would help with transport from home to church on Sundays; others would be able to offer the professional advice needed from time to time. Dr Wood was not notably a handyman and neighbours were to rally to his assistance. His Cliff College secretary, Alison Cartwright and her family were to become valued friends too - to take the place, if that could be, of family which was otherwise denied.

The years spent in Sheffield were happy and relaxed. Arthur and Mary were able to spend more time together. Coach trips were a favourite pastime and such excursions always produced a fund of anecdotes. It had been Dr Wood's practice for many years to devote Wednesday and Saturday afternoons to being with Mary, and that commitment continued in companionship and mutual encouragement until Mary died.

At her bedside in the hospital ward Arthur opened his Bible to read. His choice of scripture was Psalm 63 - 'Because you have been my help, therefore in the shadow of your wings I will rejoice. My soul follows close behind you. Your right hand upholds me.'

It was almost one year later that Arthur Wood followed Mary into the presence of the Lord. He died peacefully in the same ward at the Royal Hallamshire Hospital, Sheffield, on 28th January 1993 in the 77th year of his life. And so it was that Arthur Skevington Wood's travelling days were done.

A coach tour for Dr and Mrs Wood in retirement

ON REFLECTION

'I do not say the Glory of God is to be my first
or principle consideration but my only one!'

John Wesley

The significance of a man's life consists of more than the sum of all that he has done. It is more to do with what a man is in himself than what he has achieved. Or, as Oswald Chambers said: 'It is not what a man does that is of final importance but what a man is in what he does.' An unfortunate characteristic of the late 20th Century is that a person's accomplishments are too often, too readily and too superficially counted of great import. The character and fibre of the person, which lies sometimes hidden beneath the attainments, is usually too little recognised.

Dr Arthur Skevington Wood accomplished more than most of his contemporaries. That was partly to do with the endowment of rich and varied gifts. It was more to do with the way in which he recognised them and put them to disciplined use in the service of God. There was more to Arthur Wood than all he achieved. We look back from this vantage point in time and ask: 'What kind of man was he?'

It has been said by several who knew him well that Dr Skevington Wood was a saint, not that he would have easily recognised that description of himself or approved of such misuse of a New Testament word. He was a man who sought to fulfil the two great commandments of the Lord. He loved God with all his heart, and his love was never lukewarm. Christ had captured his mind and heart as a young man and his years of living and studying had brought his mind into captivity to Christ. The Holy Spirit filled his soul with all the fullness of God. It was from a heart set free that he spoke and wrote and lived out the grace which God had worked in him. One of his ministerial colleagues, the Revd Norman Burrows has written: 'His words were like nectar to the soul.' He lived near to God.

He loved God's people and the Church of Christ. His constant concern was that God would bring the truth of his Word to bear effectively on people's everyday lives, that they would be touched by the supernatural. Although Arthur Wood was not a man with whom it was easy to take the liberties of intimacy, he was never distant in his relationships. He had a warm heart and made friends easily. Bill Parkinson relates that on one occasion it had been asked 'Who is the easiest convention speaker to entertain in the home?' The immediate reply was, Dr Skevington Wood. He lived near to people.

His love for the church of Christ was evident in all he did. He longed for a revival to touch the church and bring new life for the glory of God. He was ecumenical in spirit in the balanced way that marked all his work. He believed passionately about a spiritual unity founded on revealed truth, but would be charitably careful about working relationships with those whose views, as he saw them, fell short of full biblical authenticity.

A man with a kindred spirit was Professor F.F. Bruce, a biblical scholar of international repute. F.F. Bruce in his book *In Retrospect* (1980) writes: 'Then, say some, would you care to comment on your reputation as a person who is always mild and restrained in criticising others?.... Much depends on what is meant by denouncing. Where someone deliberately sets himself to subvert the morals of those who are young, easily misunderstood or easily influenced, or to undermine their faith in God, no language is too severe to condemn such wickedness ... Where I consider that someone is wrong, I have no hesitation in saying so and I try to show why I consider them to be wrong (remembering that it is I who may be mistaken).' The charitable spirit of Professor Bruce is not always so clearly marked in men of much learning, though it should be, and certainly was in Dr Skevington Wood. He had a spirit which expressed itself in commending the best and correcting the worst, and always speaking the truth in love.

He loved the people of the world who, as he rightly perceived, needed to know the redemption and forgiveness offered alone in Jesus Christ. His quiet unassuming but confident personality enabled him to build bridges across the divide which separates the world from the spiritual realities of the gospel.

His saintliness was never otherworldly. His love was not mystical. Although he was not a practical man, perhaps because other priorities had taken the time which is ordinarily spent on tasks of DIY or gardening, his relationships had a practical basis. It was like this with children. Surprisingly perhaps he had a rapport with youngsters. He could take the young son of his secretary into his study to 'play at writing books.' He could enjoy watching a football match on television with children in a home in which he was staying; on one occasion, somewhat to their astonishment, 'Was a convention speaker really interested in television soccer?' they wondered. Indeed he was!

He had a warm and individualistic sense of humour. He had a twinkle in his eye as he shared some amusing anecdote, quotation, or experience with his young friends. 'Who is the preacher?' a child asked as he sat next to Dr Wood. 'The gentleman sitting next to you,' his father replied. 'I hope he doesn't preach long sermons,' the child was heard to say in rather too loud a voice. The sermon was 15 minutes long. The preacher returned to his seat with just a hint of a smile. Like his Master, he could suffer little children.

The impish sense of humour was mentioned by Dr William Davies, Principal of Cliff College, in his address at the thanksgiving service in Victoria Hall. He said: 'The last time I saw him ... he began to talk about Cliff. "When do they appoint your successor?" "Ash Wednesday," I replied. "How appropriate" he responded with a twinkle in his eye.' In his American pulpit exchange he had been surprised how listless the congregational singing had been, even of Wesley's great hymns so well known to us on this side of the Atlantic. One congregation he visited did not know 'And can it be' he wrote. He was constrained to observe, 'And can *this* be?'

One characteristic of Arthur Wood's life which all who knew him admired, was self-discipline. The Revd Howard Belben observed this when he was Principal at Cliff College and Dr Wood was a tutor. All that Arthur Wood was given to do was done expeditiously and with enthusiasm. Even if it was the work of administration, towards which he may not have been naturally disposed. Each piece of work requested of him was produced quickly and precisely.

Another, perhaps even more noticeable part of his personality, was his warmth. He felt deeply with others in their happiness or sadness. Dr Davies has written: 'Confidences he shared with me revealed his care for his students. He could laugh with them, for he had a real sense of humour ... but he could weep with them too ... and did so when occasionally one or two of them were in deep trouble ... although Arthur's tears were shed in private. He had a caring and compassionate nature.'

Arthur Skevington Wood was a humble man. He had little difficulty in regarding others better than himself. It is an open secret that he estimated his position as Principal of Cliff College quite differently from that of others. Dr William Davies has referred to a discussion with him. 'You know, I saw myself as a caretaker Principal ... ' Dr Wood had said. Arthur may have seen himself to be a caretaker Principal, but others didn't.

Indeed, he proved to be one of the most distinguished Principals Cliff College has had in its history; Dr Davies has commented. Some scholars of Dr Wood's reputation do not always see themselves in the mirror of humility, but Arthur Wood's life had been crucified with Christ, and all his achievements were evaluated in the light of the Cross, rather than in the shadows of unrefined human nature.

Dr Frederick Tatford writing rather adventurously in the Preface to *For All Seasons* expressed his own feelings towards Arthur Wood. 'One could almost wish that cloning of individuals had become practicable ... so that a myriad replicas of Skevington Wood might have been produced. But they would have been worthless without his spirituality.' More realistically, Dr Davies ended his thanksgiving service tribute with words which all can echo - 'We shall not see here on earth the like of Arthur Wood again, but his influence lives on both in his writings - and we are grateful for that legacy - and in our memories. We thank God for his life and witness.'

PART TWO

CREDO
> Dr McGonigle examines three key doctrines which marked Dr Skevington Wood as a conservative evangelical and Wesleyan.

LOVE EXCLUDING SIN
> This lecture was given by Dr Wood to the newly formed Wesley Fellowship in 1985. It represents his exposition of the distinctive Wesleyan doctrine of Sanctification.

LUTHER'S PRINCIPLES OF BIBLICAL INTERPRETATION
> Dr Wood was a Luther Scholar and this monograph first published in 1960 by Tyndale Press is reproduced by permission of Inter-Varsity Press, Leicester. It is included in this tribute to show Dr Wood's scholarly approach to historic theology from a Reformation perspective.

THE TRANSFERRED TRIUMPH
> This sermon by Dr Wood on the resurrection of Christ was discovered in manuscript after his death and is published here to illustrate the simplicity, clarity and relevance of his preaching.

CREDO
By Dr Herbert McGonigle

Throughout his long and influential life Dr Arthur Skevington Wood was happy to be known as a Methodist preacher. For him the designation 'Methodist' did not mean a narrow and partisan belonging to one denomination, rather it signified his allegiance to a historic and definable part of world-wide Evangelicalism. Cradled in a Methodist home, brought to personal faith in Christ through Methodist instrumentality and having trained for the Christian ministry at a Methodist theological college, Dr Wood was a Methodist both by experience and conviction. As Dr Rupert E. Davies has argued, Methodism has within it many schools of thought; including conservative, radical and High Church.[1] If a more precise category is sought for Dr Wood's school of theological allegiance, then it would probably have to be labelled conservative evangelical and Wesleyan. This last adjective, 'Wesleyan,' will be explained a little more fully later.

As a conservative evangelical Methodist, Dr Wood gave enthusiastic commitment to those doctrines that have always characterised evangelical Christianity. Recently Dr David Bebbington has drawn attention to what he believes to be the four leading characteristics of Evangelicalism; conversionism, activism, biblicism and crucicentrism.[2] Dr Wood would have readily identified himself with these characteristics. Evangelicalism has always given much prominence to what might be called the doctrines of grace; the inspiration and authority of Scripture, universal sinfulness, the sufficiency of Christ's atonement, regeneration through repentance and personal faith in Christ, progressive sanctification by the indwelling of the Spirit, and final judgement with eternal blessedness for the believer and eternal damnation for the unbeliever. This is not a full list of the doctrines promulgated by evangelical Christianity but it represents what evangelicals stress concerning man's salvation and final destiny.

It would be comparatively easy to illustrate each of these doctrines from the writings of Dr Wood. His special interest in Martin Luther and the Reformation, and his well-known expertise in the eighteenth-century Evangelical Revival demonstrated how the various expressions of Evangelicalism had captivated him throughout his life. Instead, however, of looking at all the evangelical doctrines that Dr Wood espoused, this chapter will concentrate on three areas of his credo that were particularly dear to his heart: Christian perfection, the nature and need of revival in the Church, and the Second Coming of Christ.

For more than sixty years John Wesley, the founder of Wesleyan Methodism, had vigorously propagated across Britain what he called scriptural holiness. By this he meant an on-going experience of God's grace in Christ that cleansed the heart of the believer from all sin and enabled him to love God and man 'with a pure heart fervently' (1 Pet. 1:22). Wesley had stressed the importance of this doctrine from as early as his 1733 sermon, The *Circumcision of the Heart*, and months before he died he wrote:

I am glad brother D   has more light with regard to full sanctification. This doctrine is the grand depositum which God has lodged with the people called Methodists; and for the sake of propagating this chiefly He appeared to have raised us up.[3]

John Wesley's life-long emphasis on this interpretation of Christian holiness has led to it becoming known as the Wesleyan understanding of sanctification, and in this sense Dr Wood was an avowed Wesleyan. Not all Methodist preachers, past or present, have been at ease with this Wesleyan credo but Dr Wood most certainly was. In English Methodism two institutions in particular have long been identified with this teaching: Cliff College and the Southport Methodist Holiness Convention. Elsewhere this tribute deals with Dr Wood's association with Cliff College, and his association with the Southport Convention was no less committed. In 1985 he published the centenary history of the Convention, *Let Us Go On*. In the Preface he wrote of how he had readily responded to the suggestion that he should research the Convention's history.

Throughout my ministry I have cherished the message of Scriptural holiness which it (the Convention) exists to proclaim. I first spoke from the Convention platform almost thirty years ago and have been a committee member since 1958....There is still a place in His purpose for its ongoing ministry.[4]

In 1967 Dr Wood published *The Burning Heart*, a thorough and meticulously-researched study of John Wesley's life and work. Seeing Wesley as primarily an evangelist, this was probably Dr Wood's most outstanding publication. He devoted an entire chapter to Wesley's teaching on entire sanctification, entitling it 'The Grand Depositum.' Carefully tracing Wesley's teaching throughout more than sixty years of writing and preaching, Dr

Wood showed what that Wesleyan distinctive was. With other evangelicals Wesley had stressed sanctification as a process of grace in the Christian life, beginning with the new birth. But John Wesley, and Dr Wood, went further. Within that process of gradual sanctification there is a crisis of faith, a crisis consequent upon evangelical repentance. This crisis of full cleansing from inner sin lifts the believer to a higher plane of spiritual victory and more rapid growth in all the graces of Christlikeness. Dr Wood argued cogently that the consequence of this experience is, in Wesley's own words: 'A Christian is so far perfect as not to commit sin.' Wesley was not saying that the entirely sanctified Christian could not sin but that in unbroken communion with Christ through the Spirit he need not sin. To make it clear that this evaluation of John Wesley's teaching on scriptural holiness represented his own convictions, Dr Wood added:

> This is the glorious privilege of every Christian. There is
> no need for him to fall into evil. He may in fact do so, but
> that is not God's will for him....The crisis of entire
> sanctification is never isolated from the process of spiritual
> development, which both precedes and follows it.[5]

When the Wesley Fellowship was launched in 1985 with its declared aim of seeking to promote 'the distinctive teaching and doctrine of the historic Wesleyan expression' of the Christian faith, Dr Wood enthusiastically joined it. Asked to deliver the Fellowship's first 'Occasional Paper,' not surprisingly he chose as his subject, *Love Excluding Sin*, with the subtitle, 'Wesley's Doctrine of Sanctification.' Within twenty-four pages, including one hundred and thirty one references, he produced one of the best-ever short treatments of Wesley's teaching. With his unrivalled knowledge of Wesley's writings and what has been written since in this field by Wesley's theological friends and opponents, Dr Wood was well equipped to present a definitive statement. He showed first how Wesley saw sanctification as the optimism of grace in the Christian life. God wants his people to be holy and he has made full provision for their holiness. Secondly, Dr Wood examined Wesley's exposition of the doctrine, and then concluded by drawing attention to Wesley's distinctive insights that have helped in the understanding of sanctification since his day. Though not concluding that John Wesley's exposition of the selected biblical texts was beyond censure in every instance or that he had said the last word on entire sanctification, Dr Wood, nevertheless, gave unequivocal allegiance to Wesley's basic exposition.

Wesley was not only in line with the Reformation but also an heir of the Puritans....His doctrine expressed the optimism of grace with regard to the believer's deliverance from sin. This means deliverance from inward as well as outward sin....Wesley's outlook was existential. His was the theology of the present moment. In this moment the believer may be free from sin....If this moment, why not the next and indeed every moment?[6]

A second characteristic of Dr Wood's credo was his on-going interest in the principles of spiritual revival. While a study of revival may not be a single, precisely-stated, doctrine of evangelical Christianity, yet it presumes within itself the basic doctrines of sin, grace and salvation. Dr Wood's intense interest in the sixteenth-century German Reformation and the British and American eighteenth-century Awakening was expressive of his interest in revival. He saw Martin Luther raised up by God to revive the Church of his day by bringing it back to the essential New Testament experience of salvation by faith. He saw John and Charles Wesley similarly raised of God to herald revival in their times. But the work of the Wesley brothers did not represent the whole work of God in that century. Dr Wood's study, *The Inextinguishable Blaze*, published in 1960, is among the best-researched and documented accounts of the spiritual renewal experienced in Britain and America in the eighteenth century.

It was immediately after the Dr Billy Graham crusades in England in 1954 and 1955, crusades which Dr Wood warmly supported, that he turned his attention deliberately to an investigation of the phenomenon of revival in Scripture and Church history. The fruit of this investigation was his 1958 book, *And With Fire*, republished in 1981 as *Baptised With Fire*, and subtitled 'God Promises Revival.' Having examined some of the more important definitions of revival that Church historians have advanced, he did not offer his own precise definition of revival but argued instead its leading characteristics.

Revival is a many-splendoured thing and can no more be confined to a formula than the grace of God....It comes from above. It is received by the openness of faith. It produces salvation and righteousness....The final objective of revival is to magnify the majesty and mercy of our incomparable Redeemer.[7]

Dr Wood was convinced by both the Scripture passages and the historical evidence that revival was the purpose of God for his

Church and therefore all Christians should work and pray, long for and expect revival. He agreed with John Bonar that a revival 'is but multiplied conversions,' it is 'but living Christianity.' If we don't need conversion, if we don't need Christ, if our children and friends and neighbours do not need the grace of regeneration, then we don't need revival. 'But if conversion is necessary, if regeneration is necessary, if salvation is necessary, then is a revival necessary.'

Writing on 'The Marks of a Revival,' Dr Wood set out first what a revival is not. It is independent of organisation, not being a stunt, or a publicity project or even a well-planned evangelistic crusade. It is also independent of personalities. God often uses men and women for his purpose but God Himself is 'the sovereign originator of all revival.' And revival is independent of evangelism. This is not to decry evangelism but rather to distinguish between the on-going challenge to the Church to evangelise the lost and a Pentecostal cloudburst that creates a flood of spiritual blessing and sweeps men and women into the Kingdom in unprecedented numbers. 'When the Church takes the Gospel to the people that is evangelism. When the people come to the Church for the Gospel, that is revival.'[8]

Having set out what revival is not, Dr Wood then proceeded to show its five positive and distinctive features. These are: agonised praying, a new awareness and recognition of God, brokenness and humility before him, and openness to God, and, finally, a faithfulness and devotion to God's holy will. But Dr Wood was not content to argue and illustrate and reference these distinctives of revival. He longed fervently to witness them in his own heart and among fellow Christians. This spiritual son of John Wesley was no mere disinterested hagiographer or dry-as-dust historian; he was an evangelist and a soul-winner with a personal passion for revival.

> We have space only to mention [these] five great marks of revival in every age. Pray over them. Agonise about them. Shed tears for them. Plead with God that these may once again become the signs following the Word within Christ's Church.[9]

Finally, Dr Arthur Skevington Wood had an intense interest in biblical prophecy. That subject needs immediate qualification for the bare mention of prophecy is a reminder of the many extravagant claims, counter-claims, predictions and forecasts, made by dispensationalists, pre- and post- millennialists, tribulationists and a host of chiliast advocates inside and outside historic Evangelicalism. By contrast Dr Wood's writing and preaching on this topic was marked by careful biblical exegesis and sound exposition and application. His understanding of biblical prophecy focussed particularly on Christ's Second Coming. By this he meant that just as surely as Christ had come into our world in person in the Incarnation, so he will come again in power and great glory at his Parousia or Second Coming. When the New Testament speaks of this event, Dr Wood argued, it does not merely mean that Christ comes by his Spirit to every believer, or that Christ comes constantly to renew and bless his Church or that he will come and receive the soul of the believer at the moment of death. Rather it means he will come in visible glory and power to bring about the end of the age, translate his Church to heaven, judge the nations and set up his Kingdom on earth. Although not dogmatic on the order of these events, yet Dr Wood was sure that anything less than an avowal of Christ's Second Coming and related doctrines was to ignore plain New Testament teaching.

Invited to deliver the 1991 annual Maynard James Memorial Lecture, Dr Wood chose as his subject, *Third Wave or Second Coming*, subtitled, 'The Relevance of Biblical Prophecy.' He asserted that a large part of Scripture is concerned with predictive prophecy. As the Old Testament pointed forwards to the first coming of Christ, so many passages in the New Testament point forward to his Second Coming. Dr Wood's prophetic hermeneutic gave little attention to theories about the length of the Tribulation, the identification of the beast and the antichrist and what roles will be played in the prophetic drama by Israel and the other nations of the Middle East. Instead he concentrated on six reasons for giving serious attention to the prophetic word concerning the Second Coming of Christ.

First, it makes sense of history. The final destiny of the world and mankind is not in the hands of evil tyrants or left to the vagaries of chance or fortune. God is in control and in his time, Christ will return to earth and all history will find its consummation in his return and the establishment of his eternal Kingdom.

Secondly, biblical prophecy attests the reliability of Scripture. Just as some three hundred Old Testament predictions were fulfilled in the birth, life, death and resurrection of Christ, so the New Testament's three hundred references to his Second Coming can be expected to be fulfilled with the same certainty. In an age of scepticism about the whole idea of divine revelation in the

Bible, Dr Wood was sure that prophecy fulfilled and prophecy yet to be fulfilled pointed to the divine origin of the Scriptures.

Thirdly, the prophetic word gives believers assurance about the future. Christ will come again and rapture both the believing dead and the living saints. That great event will trigger the other great consequent events; the world's last clash of arms at Armageddon, the inauguration of Christ's millennial reign on earth, the judgement of the great white throne, and, finally, the eternal states of blessedness for the believer and eternal ruin for the unbeliever. Dr Wood made it clear that he unhesitatingly believed these doctrines to be the teaching of the New Testament, and that believing these truths gives the Christian unshakeable confidence in God's purposes and plans.

Fourthly, this prophetic emphasis should prompt all Christians to a new urgency in evangelism. While not lessening the biblical teaching on the love of God for a lost world, Dr Wood was in no doubt that the day of grace will end suddenly when Christ returns. Although he refused to speculate about dates and would never have attempted a prophetic timetable, he was sure that the end of the Church age was not far away. That conviction should stir us to work for the salvation of souls while the day of opportunity is still with us. And Dr Wood did not hesitate to declare his convictions about the fate of the unbeliever.

The Christians of the apostolic age were convinced, as we should be, that those who were not saved at the return of Christ would be damned eternally. In these tolerant, sentimental times, it is unfashionable to dwell on such solemn themes, but they are dealt with in God's Word and we dare not shut our eyes to them.[10]

Fifthly, Dr Wood stressed the importance of biblical prophecy teaching in calling all believers to a life of holiness. He drew attention to the many New Testament passages where the hope of Christ's return is made an incentive for holy living. All those who expect their Lord to return to earth in power and glory must live in readiness for that return. In this way the Christian hope and the Christian life are inextricably bound together in Scripture. Only those who follow after holiness will see the Lord when he returns (Heb. 12:14).

Finally, the New Testament teaching on Christ's Second Coming directs our attention to the incomparable glory, majesty and authority of our Lord Jesus Christ. He will come again, every eye will see him, and his glory, hidden through the ages, will fill the worlds with wonder and reverence. When Christ is crowned with many crowns, every knee will bow to him and every tongue confess that he 'is Lord to the glory of God the Father' (Rev. 19:12; Phil. 2:10,11).

As already indicated, this brief look at Dr Wood's credo touches on only three of those evangelical doctrines that he believed and propagated so fervently. Not all evangelicals, not even all his fellow Methodists, would share these emphases in detail. But all who knew Dr Arthur Skevington Wood through friendship, hearing him preach or reading his publications, knew him to be an unashamed, Bible-believing evangelical. This chapter has sought to demonstrate that in his faith he was an ardent advocate of scriptural holiness, a promoter of revival and renewal in the Church, and a prophetic voice calling Christians to live and work and witness in the light of Christ's Second Coming.

REFERENCES

1 R.E. Davies, *What Methodists Believe* (Epworth Press, 1989), p. V.
2 D.W. Bebbington, *Evangelicalism in Modern Britain* (Unwin Hyman, 1989), pp. 5-17.
3 J. Wesley, *Letters* Vol. 8, p. 238.
4 A.S. Wood, *Let Us Go On* (Moorleys, 1985), p. 5.
5 A.S. Wood, *The Burning Heart* (Paternoster Press, 1967), pp. 268, 269.
6 A.S. Wood, *Love Excluding Sin* (Moorleys for the Wesley Fellowship, 1986), pp. 17, 18.
7 A.S. Wood, *Baptised With Fire* (Pickering and Inglis, 1981), pp. 39, 49.
8 Ibid., p. 86.
9 Ibid., p. 87.
10 A.S. Wood, *Third Wave or Second Coming?* (Moorleys for the Wesley Fellowship, 1991), p. 18.

LOVE EXCLUDING SIN
JOHN WESLEY'S TEACHING ON SANCTIFICATION
by Dr Skevington Wood

A prominent feature of current scholarly investigation in the Church historical field is a reassessment of John Wesley's contribution to theology. Too often in the past he has been dismissed as something of a lightweight in this department. Since his major role was that of an itinerant evangelist and the spearhead of revival, it has been assumed that his theological significance is comparatively minimal. While recognizing that Wesley's preoccupations prevented him from spending long hours in research or in producing some definitive doctrinal exposition, it is being realized that his theology, hammered out as it was on the anvil of practical experience and at times of keen controversy, possessed a value that has hitherto been largely unappreciated.

The verdict of Bishop Ole Borgen is representative of contemporary estimates. 'John Wesley was a clear-thinking, well-read theologian. True, if by "theology" we mean speculative systems elaborately spun out in learned volumes, Wesley was not a great theologian. He wrote no *Summa* or systematic theology. But underlying and undergirding all his preaching, writing and action was a solid theological structure which enabled the Revival to weather the many theological storms of eighteenth century England.'[1]

If Wesley's contribution to theology has been underestimated until very recently, his distinctive stance is still regularly and seriously misapprehended. He is classed all too often as an Arminian of the Laudian and Latitudinarian variety, associated with the English Church in the seventeenth century, as if his position was virtually indistinguishable from semi-Pelagianism. It needs to be stressed that the experiential and theological crisis of Wesley's evangelical conversion in 1738 represented a rejection of the humanistic Arminianism of so much Anglican teaching and preaching in the eighteenth century and an acceptance of the reformed emphasis on the necessity for justification by faith which was as central to the theology of Arminius as to that of Luther and Calvin. Wesley, then, was an evangelical Arminian in the line of Arminius himself, the essence of whose protest against the extremes of supralapsarianism (see p. 73.) lay in the application of the Protestant principle of *sola gratia*. Wesley's theology is fundamentally orthodox and evangelical. As Professor

W.R. Cannon has summarized it, his anthropology is thoroughly Augustinian with a few minor modifications; his doctrine of God is that of the Thirty Nine Articles; his exaltation of the atonement in its objective signification is as high and as splendid as Anselm's and his dependence on divine grace is as absolute as Calvin's.[2] It is against this background of biblically orientated traditionalism that Wesley's doctrine of sanctification must be set. The case history hardly leads us to anticipate eccentricities. In his teaching on this, and on every other subject, Wesley's aim was to present Scriptural Christianity, as the reformers sought to do.

It is clear that Wesley regarded sanctification as being of cardinal importance in theology and even more in experience. He had no interest in a theology that was unrelated to life. Abstractions made no appeal to him. 'Our main doctrines, which include all the rest, are three, - that of repentance, of faith, and of holiness' - this is from *The Principles of a Methodist Farther Explained* (1746). 'The first of these we account, as it were, the porch of religion; the next the door; the third religion itself'.[3] When in 1763 Wesley attempted to form an Evangelical Alliance of Anglican clergymen involved in the revival, he invited all who agreed in three essentials: 1. Original Sin; 2. Justification by Faith; 3. Holiness of Heart and Life, with this characteristic codicil: 'provided their life be answerable to their doctrine'.[4]

1. We begin by considering Wesley's basic understanding of sanctification. His approach represents a reaction against restrictive views which seemed to limit the scope of what God can do in a life that is altogether devoted to him. A French writer, Laurent Etienne Rondet, has referred to what he calls a 'pessimism of grace' - a one-sided seventeenth century reinterpretation of Augustinian and reformed anthropology which so stressed the effects of sin as to make the fall rather than the cross and resurrection the real pivot of history.[5] Not only did such an outlook inhibit the expectation of any considerable response on the part of sinful man to the offer of salvation: it also cramped the work of sanctification by allowing the principle of sin to play an unduly prominent role in the experience of the believer. Wesley, on the other hand, represented an 'optimism of grace' in relation to the extent of salvation, both in terms of its initial reception and its continuing effect in progressive holiness. In his sermon 'On Perfection' (1788), Wesley quoted the divine command recorded in 1 Peter 1:15 - 'Be ye holy, as he that hath called you is holy in all manner of conversation' - and explained that it 'implies a promise that we shall be thus holy, if we are not

wanting to ourselves. Nothing can be wanting on God's part: as he has called us to holiness, he is undoubtedly willing, as well as able to work this holiness in us. For he cannot mock his helpless creatures, calling us to receive what he never intends to give. That he does call us to it is undeniable; therefore he will give it if we are not disobedient to the heavenly calling.'[6]

Wesley's understanding of sanctification places it firmly in the context of total salvation. Sanctification is no postscript or appendix to the overall scheme of redemption. It is no extraneous factor, representing some private obsession on the part of the Wesleys. As Dr Franz Hildebrandt justifiably contends, 'Methodism has no pet doctrine: it goes out for the whole of the New Testament.'[7] For John Wesley, as indeed for his brother, that wholeness included the full implications of what God purposes to bring about in the life of the sanctified. His concern was for what he described in a pastoral letter as 'the whole Christian salvation'.[8] This comprehensive use of the term was intended to include the entire range of salvation, from the believer's initial deliverance from sin, through the ongoing process of sanctification or full salvation, to that consummation in glory which is final salvation. Here was how the matter was resolved at the Conference of 1746. 'In asserting salvation by faith we mean this: (1) That pardon (salvation begun) is received by faith producing works. (2) That holiness (salvation continued) is faith working by love. (3) That heaven (salvation finished) is the reward of this faith.'[9]

More usually, however, Wesley has present salvation in mind: namely, the outworking (in an advancing experience of grace) of a salvation already received. He told one of his preachers, Samuel Bardsley, that if he desired the work of God to deepen in believers, he should 'continually exhort them to go on unto perfection, steadily to use all the grace they have received, and every moment to expect full salvation.'[10] In his *Farther Appeal to Men of Reason and Religion* (1748) Wesley clarified his position with admirable conciseness. 'By salvation I mean, not barely, according to the vulgar notion, deliverance from hell, or going to heaven; but a present deliverance from sin, a restoration of the soul to its primitive health, its original purity; a recovery of the divine nature; the renewal of our souls after the image of God, in righteousness and true holiness, in justice, mercy and truth. This implies all holy and heavenly tempers, and, by consequence, all holiness of conversation.'[11] From such a biblical account of what salvation involves he was able to draw a significant conclusion.

'Now, if by salvation we mean a present salvation from sin, we cannot say, holiness is the condition of it: for it is the thing itself. Salvation, in this sense, and holiness, are synonymous terms.' [12] Viewed in the total context of salvation, sanctification was seen by Wesley as the work of God in the soul of man from the moment of justification to the moment of physical death. As Harald Lindström explains, 'it comprises the whole process of recovery, the object of which is to restore man to the image of God. This is the widest but also the most proper use of the word sanctification. It is also one that corresponds best to Wesley's idea of the factual significance of sanctification.' [13] But Wesley also used the word in a narrower sense to describe a specific stage and resultant condition within the process of general sanctification. This he distinguished as full or entire sanctification. We propose to discuss the gradual and instantaneous aspects of the experience later in this paper. For the moment, however, we must take note of Wesley's double emphasis. Too often Wesley's doctrine of sanctification has been treated solely in terms of this second and indeed secondary understanding of it, forgetting that the basis of his teaching and its major thrust is related to the concept of development.

How did Wesley define this doctrine? As he sought to commend it in his preaching and writing, there are certain phrases which recur with some degree of regularity. It is to these that we must turn if we are to discover what he meant by sanctification or holiness. Put at its simplest, it was to be a Christian, a complete Christian, a fully-equipped Christian, a Christian as Christ wants us to be and undertakes to make us. It is not to be an élitist or eccentric Christian, for the New Testament approves no such categories. It is to realize the full potential of God's provision. Wesley was sufficiently uncomplicated in mind to discern the fundamental nature of sanctification in this obvious but frequently neglected sense. Certainly the eighteenth century Church needed to be recalled from its more abstruse philosophical speculations, let alone destructive rationalistic criticism, to face the pressingly pragmatic question of what it really means to be a Christian. It was with this enquiry that Wesley dared to face one of the leading controversialists of his day - Dr Conyers Middleton, Fellow of Trinity College, Cambridge, who in his *Letter to Dr Waterland* (1731) and *Free Enquiry* (1749) had struck successive blows at the supernatural origins of the Christian faith. [14] Having submitted the latter volume to an exacting scrutiny, running to some sixty pages in the standard edition of his letters, Wesley raised what for him was the paramount issue. 'We have long been disputing about Christians, about Christianity, and the evidence whereby it is supported. But what do these terms mean? Who is a Christian indeed? What is real, genuine Christianity? And what is the surest and most accessible evidence (if I may so speak) whereby I may know it is of God?'[15]

Here was Wesley coming to the point with typical directness. Incidentally we cannot fail to be impressed, as was Professor George Croft Cell, with Wesley's strikingly modern way of approaching the matter.[16] The second of his questions, somewhat abbreviated, comprised the title of Adolf Harnack's Berlin lectures in 1900. In the preface to *What is Christianity?* Harnack paid his respects to theologians who do no more than 'treat of the Gospel in the recondite language of learning and bury it in scholarly folios.'[17] That was precisely Wesley's attitude. He was anxious to answer the practical question, 'Who is a Christian?'

In the preface to the third volume of *Hymns and Sacred Poems*, published in 1742, Wesley spoke of the 'perfect man, sanctified throughout,' as 'one in whom is "the mind which was in Christ", and who so 'walketh as Christ also walked"'.[18] The combination of these two New Testament references crystallizes his definition. This, he told a correspondent, is 'the Bible *method* of salvation' and 'the very essence of Christian perfection'.[19] In the *Farther Appeal* he referred to our Lord's insistence on that 'righteousness which exceeds the righteousness of the Scribes and Pharisees' without which we cannot 'enter the kingdom of heaven', - 'even the life of God in the soul; holiness of heart, producing all holiness of conversation' or behaviour.[20] As far back as 1739 Wesley had spoken similarly in his *Journal*. He dissociated himself from the formalism of those clergy who regarded sanctification merely as a matter of externals. 'I believe it to be an inward thing,' he claimed, 'namely, the life of God in the soul of man; a participation in the divine nature; the mind that was in Christ; or, the renewal of our heart after the image of him that created us'.[21] *The Life of God in the Soul of Man* (1677) was the title of a devotional book written by Henry Scougal of Aberdeen to which Wesley had been introduced by his mother who valued it even above Richard Baxter's *The Saints' Everlasting Rest* (1650).[22] It also influenced George Whitefield.[23]

In the sermon 'On Perfection' Wesley showed that when the apostle Paul invites the Ephesians to put on 'the new man, which is created after God, in righteousness and true holiness' (4:24), or reminds the Colossians that they have already put on 'the new man which is renewed in knowledge after the image of him that created him' (3:10), the allusion is plainly to the creation of man as recorded in Genesis 1:27.[24] 'Now the moral image of God consists (as the apostle observes) "in righteousness and true holiness". By sin this is totally destroyed. And we never can recover it, till we are "created anew in Christ Jesus". And this is perfection'.[25] In his *Answer* to the erratic William Dodd in 1756, Wesley took perfection to be 'only another term for holiness, or the image of God in man', and defended the equation against the objections of his correspondent.[26]

The stress on sanctification as being an inward disposition is consistently reiterated in Wesley's writings. 'Perfection is another name for universal holiness', he claimed, after appealing to 1 Peter 1:15; and then proceeded to define it as 'inward and outward righteousness: holiness of life arising from holiness of heart'.[27] Wesley would have been the last to decry the need for external evidence. Inner sanctification will manifest itself in outward conduct. But being a Christian is not an imitation of externals. It is essentially an affair of the heart. It was the Pharisees who concentrated on surface cleansing. Jesus went deeper in his demands. 'Outward religion without inward is nothing', Wesley declared as he pleaded with those who were 'posting to hell, and fancying it was heaven'.[28] (see p. 73.) Indeed, he went on, it 'is far worse than nothing, being, indeed, no other than a solemn mockery of God'.[29] Even the 'inward conviction of our wants is nothing, unless those wants are in fact supplied. Good desires also are nothing, unless we actually attain what we are stirred up to desire'.[30]

The inwardness of sanctification is understood as involving purity. In the *Plain Account of Christian Perfection* (1766), Wesley described the 'one that is perfect' as a man 'that hath clean hands and a pure heart', or that is 'cleansed from all filthiness of flesh and spirit'.[31] 'To declare this a little more particularly: we understand by that scriptural expression, "a perfect man", one in whom God hath fulfilled his faithful word, "From all your filthiness and from all your idols I will cleanse you: I will also save you from all your uncleannesses." We understand hereby one whom God hath "sanctified throughout in body, soul and spirit", one who "walketh in the light as he is in the light, in whom is no darkness at all; the blood of Jesus Christ his Son having cleansed him from all sin"'.[32] In the sermon on 'Original Sin' (1759) Wesley employed the analogy of physical healing. The proper nature of religion he said is therapeia psychĕs - 'God's method of healing a soul which is thus diseased (i.e. by the infection of sin). Hereby the great Physician of souls applies medicines to heal this sickness: to restore human nature, totally corrupted in all its faculties'.[33] The outcome of such cleansing, healing and deliverance is liberty. Holiness is emancipation. The Christian is one who enjoys release from the tensions of circumstance and sin. 'Perfect love and Christian liberty are the very same thing,' Wesley told Joseph Benson, 'and those two expressions are equally proper, being equally scriptural... What is Christian liberty but another word for holiness?'[34] Freedom from the guilt of sin and the fear of hell are so far from being the whole of Christian liberty, however, that they are 'the least and lowest part'.[35] The major emancipation is 'from the power of sin, from serving the devil, from offending God.[36]

In the sermon 'On Perfection', Wesley defined his subject as 'the one undivided fruit of the Spirit,' as expounded by Paul in Galatians 5: 22,23.[37] 'What a glorious constellation of graces is here!' Wesley exclaimed. 'Now suppose all these to be knit together in one, to be united together in the soul of a believer, this is Christian perfection.'[38] But precisely this is God's goal for man and the purpose for which the Holy Spirit has been bestowed. Wesley conceded that the reception of the Spirit does not now reproduce all the supernaturally miraculous effects which accompanied the initial gift at Pentecost. But Christians nevertheless do still receive and are in fact filled with the Spirit in order to be filled with the fruit of the Spirit.[39] The Spirit 'inspires into all true believers now, a degree of the same peace and joy and love which the apostles felt themselves on that day of Pentecost.'[40]

Sanctification is identified by Wesley with simplicity of intention - an undivided concentration on pleasing and obeying God. In 1789 he published a sermon, 'On a Single Eye' from our Lord's words in Matthew 6:22,23. He quoted Thomas à Kempis, Jeremy Taylor and William Law from whom many years before he had learned this particular aspect of holiness.[41] Simplicity of intention means having 'one design and one desire.'[42] It is to know God, to love him, to serve him, and to glorify him. It embraces enjoying 'God in all, and above all things in time and in eternity.'[44]

Wesley's construction of sanctification found its focus and climax in love. 'True Christian perfection', he announced, 'is no other than humble love.'[45] 'What is implied in being a perfect

Christian?' was one of the questions asked when the doctrine was discussed at the first Methodist conference in 1744.[46] This was the answer given: 'The loving the Lord our God with all our heart, and with all our mind, and soul, and strength (Deut. 6:5; 30:6; Ezek. 36:25-9).'[47] In his sermon 'On Patience,' Wesley insisted that 'love is the sum of Christian sanctification.'[48] 'Holiness is none other than pure love,' he assured Mrs Bennis, 'a heart devoted to God, one design and one desire.'[49] 'What I mean by perfection I have defined both in the first and the *Farther Thoughts* upon that subject,' he reminded John Fletcher: 'pure love, rejoicing evermore, praying always, in everything giving thanks.'[50] 'All that is necessarily implied therein (i.e. in Christian Perfection),' he explained to Hannah Ball, the pioneer of Methodist Sunday Schools, 'is humble, gentle, patient love, love regulating all the tempers and governing all the words and actions.'[51] He advised Ann Loxdale frequently to read and meditate upon the thirteenth Chapter of 1 Corinthians. There is the true picture of Christian Perfection! Let us copy after it with all our might.[52] When Henry Venn, the evangelical Rector of Huddersfield, charged him with proclaiming perfection, Wesley admitted that he did. 'True - that is, loving God with *all* our heart, and serving him with *all* our strength. I teach nothing more, nothing less than this.'[53]

Wesley's understanding of sanctification was nowhere made more explicit than in his definitive sermon on 'The Scripture Way of Salvation' 1765). He spoke of entire sanctification, of expressions like 'full salvation' and 'perfection' as used in the letter to the Hebrews. 'But what is perfection? The word has various senses: here it means perfect love. It is love excluding sin; love filling the heart, taking up the whole capacity of the same.'[54] That statement is confirmed in a letter to Walter Churchey in 1771. 'Entire sanctification, or Christian perfection, is neither more nor less than pure love - love expelling sin and governing both the heart and life of a child of God. The Refiner's fire purges out all that is contrary to love, and that many times by a pleasing smart. Leave all this to him that does all things well and that loves you better than you do yourself.'[55] The expression is even found in Wesley's admonitory charge to the errant Thomas Maxfield. He had been drawn away by the fanaticism of one of Wesley's itinerants, George Bell, a disciple of Robert Sandeman, the Scottish sectarian who taught an exaggerated and unscriptural perfectionism which asserted that man could reach a stage of angelic sinlessness. Nevertheless,

Wesley could at least agree with Maxfield's basic premise, that perfection is 'pure love; love excluding sin.'[56] In what sense pure love may exclude or expel sin was to be carefully expounded by Wesley as he confronted those who took his teaching to extremes which he himself could never countenance.

'Love' - 'pure love' - 'love expelling sin' - 'perfect love': these were the designations Wesley employed to express the quintessence of sanctification. 'Christian perfection' was not one of his choices. 'I have no particular fondness for the term', he explained to Dr Dodd. 'It is my opponents who thrust it upon me continually, and ask me what I mean by it.'[57] Perfection, on the other hand, (as distinct from Christian perfection) is found in the vocabulary of Scripture and no-one ought therefore to object to its use whatever they may think of the way in which it is interpreted by some.[58] 'As to *the word*, it is scriptural', Wesley pointed out to Martin Madan's sister, Penelope Maitland, 'therefore neither you nor I can in conscience object against it, unless we would send the Holy Ghost to school and teach him to speak who made the tongue.'[59] In similar vein Wesley cautioned Samuel Furly: 'Stop! you must not cavil at that word (i.e. perfection): you are not wiser than the Holy Ghost. But if you are not, see that you teach perfection too.'[60] And in the *Earnest Appeal* he reduced the problem to its unadorned essentials: 'Have you not another objection..... namely, that we preach perfection? True: but what perfection? The term you cannot object to, because it is scriptural. All the difficulty is, to fix the meaning of it according to the Word of God. And this we have done again and again.'[61]

2. Having considered Wesley's basic understanding of sanctification, we must proceed to look more closely at his exposition of this doctrine. With a realistic sense of balance, which is altogether typical of his outlook, he warned against the danger of taking either too exalted or too reductionist a view of the matter. 'My judgement is... that to overdo is to undo, and that to set perfection too high (so high as no man we ever heard or read of attained) is the most effectual (because unsuspected) way of driving it out of the world.'[62] John Wesley felt that even his brother Charles strayed in this direction and did not hesitate to tell him so. 'I still think to set perfection *so high* is effectually to renounce it.'[63] On the other hand, Wesley sought to avoid any lowering of the ethical and spiritual standard. In reply to William Dodd, he made his position plain. 'Nor did I ever say or mean any *more* by perfection than *thus* loving and serving God. But I dare not say *less* than this, for it might be attended with

worse consequences than you seem to be aware of. If there be a mistake, it is far more dangerous on the one side than on the other. If I set the work too high, I drive men into needless fears; if you set it too low, you drive them into hell fire.'[64]

In his sermon on 'Christian Perfection' composed at the instigation of Edmund Gibson, Bishop of London, who encouraged him to publicize his views, Wesley set out to show in what sense Christians are not and in what sense they are perfect.[65] His text was Philippians 3:12, 'Not as though I had already attained, either were already perfect.' We shall adopt his own negative and positive treatment as we deal first with Wesley's negative safeguards and then with his positive insights.

In controversy both with the Sandemanian ultra-perfectionists who advocated an idealistic but impracticable angelism, and the latitudinarian indifferentists who complained that the sanctification he proclaimed represented an impossible and unnecessary standard, Wesley found himself constantly rebutting misinformed accusations about what he was reputed to teach. Much of his time was taken up with clearing the ground for a more positive statement by first of all explaining what perfection is not. Paradoxical as it may seem, and inconsistent as it sometimes was if we compare Wesley's *ad hoc* comments with one another, he was striving to arrive at a concept of perfection which still made allowances for considerable imperfection. To a certain extent this arose from his failure to interpret perfection biblically in terms of maturity rather than finished flawlessness. But to the last Wesley endeavoured to safeguard his teaching from misunderstanding and undue exaggeration by hedging it about with qualifying negatives. This is apparent from his important reply to Henry Venn, whose hesitations about Wesley's doctrine of sanctification arose neither from enthusiastic extremism nor from insipid moderatism, but from his Calvinistic convictions. Having defined Christian perfection in terms of pure love, Wesley added: 'And whatever infirmity, default, *anomia*, is consistent with this any man may teach, and I shall not contradict him.'[66] That was partly because Wesley regarded the interpretation of holiness as an area of toleration and not as a rigid article of faith, but also because he himself was prepared to accommodate anything short of wilful, habitual sin to his notion of perfection. 'I believe that a truly sanctified person does involuntarily fall short in divers instances of the rule marked out in the Thirteenth Chapter to the Corinthians,' he confessed to Samuel Furly.[67] Urging an influential patroness, Miss Marsh, to hold fast to a scriptural account of perfection as the fullness of love, he immediately introduced a proviso. 'But then remember, on the other hand, you have this treasure in an earthen vessel; you dwell in a poor, shattered house of clay, which presses down the immortal spirit. Hence all your thoughts, words and actions are so imperfect, so far from coming up to the standard (that law of love, which, but for the corruptible body, your soul would answer in all instances), that you may well say till you go to him you love, "Every moment, Lord, I need The merit of thy death."'[68]

Wesley was disarmingly frank in admitting the logical incongruity of an imperfect perfection. 'I know not how to reconcile speaking sharply or roughly, or even a seeming want of meekness with perfection and yet I am fearful of condemning whom God has not condemned. What I cannot understand I leave to him.'[69] We detect a certain naivety in Wesley's assessment of personal testimonies to the experience of sanctification. He was prepared to give some of his fellow Methodists the benefit of more than one doubt. Perhaps like Herodotus, the father of history, his weakness lay in a streak of credulity.

Wesley consistently maintained that the perfection he preached was *not absolute*. That belongs only to God. Any perfection man may attain is derived and relative. Wesley strongly dissented from the suggestion of George Bell and the extremists who taught that man can be absolutely perfect. 'I never contended for it', he assured Penelope Maitland.[70] He was equally adamant that perfection is *not angelic*. Preaching late in his life on Hebrews 6:1 - 'Let us go on to perfection' - he undertook to demonstrate the nature of perfection initially in terms of negative exclusions. He made this his starting point. Since the angels never 'left their first estate', all their original faculties remain unimpaired. Their apprehension is always clear and their judgement always true. Though their knowledge is limited, since they are created beings, they are not liable to error. Their actions are aligned to their inerrant understanding so that they invariably perform the good and acceptable will of God. 'Therefore it is not possible for man, whose understanding is darkened, to whom mistake is as natural as ignorance; who cannot think at all, but by the mediation of organs which are weakened and depraved, like the other parts of his corruptible body; it is not possible, I say, for men always to think right, to apprehend things distinctly, and to judge truly of them. In consequence hereof, his affections, depending on his understanding, are variously disordered. And his words and actions are influenced, more or less, by the disorder both of his understanding and affections. It follows that no man, while in the body, can possibly attain to angelic perfection.[71.]

In the same sermon, Wesley showed that perfection is *not Adamic*. That is to say, it is not to be confused with that which applied to Adam prior to the fall. Adam was as pure and free from sin as the angels themselves. His understanding and judgement, his motivation and actions, were as impeccable as theirs. Since man rebelled against God, argued Wesley, the case is widely different with him.[72] He is no longer able to avoid falling into innumerable mistakes. He cannot always feel, think, speak and act aright. Consequently, Wesley concluded, man in his present condition can no more attain Adamic than angelic perfection.[73] Lindström has set out Wesley's contrast between Adamic and Christian perfection in tabular form.[74] Adamic perfection is based on the covenant of works: man must fulfil the law of works. Christian perfection is based on the covenant of grace: man must fulfil the law of faith.

Adamic perfection signifies perfect obedience to every point in this law. Holiness must be perfect in degree and continue without intermission through the whole life. Christian perfection signifies perfect obedience insofar as this is obtainable in the present circumstances of man. It means perfect love. Holiness is a perfection of nature, not of degree. It concerns man's will and intention. Adamic perfection is moreover a perfect fulfilment of the law and perfect deliverance from sin in the relative and subjective sense. The qualifications attached to the concept of Christian perfection as over against that of Adam go some way, at least, to account for the apparent ambivalence of Wesley's teaching. There is a sense in which he recognized that Christian perfection is at best imperfect in view of the conditions under which man now lives since Adam's fateful transgression.

If sanctification, then, is regarded by Wesley as that which is possible for fallen man, with all his built-in limitations and frailties, it is clearly *not infallible*. He strenuously denied that he ever suggested that man may be so holy as to be faultless. 'The highest perfection which man can attain, while the soul dwells in the body, does not exclude ignorance, and error, and a thousand other infirmities. Now, from wrong judgements, wrong words and actions will necessarily flow. And in some cases wrong affections also may spring from the same source. I may judge wrong of you; I may think more or less highly of you than I ought to think; and this mistake in my judgement may not only occasion something wrong in my behaviour but it may have a still deeper effect; it may occasion something wrong in my affection. From a wrong apprehension, I may love and esteem you either more or less than I ought. Nor can I be freed from a liableness to such a mistake while I remain in a corruptible body. A thousand infirmities, in consequence of this, will attend my spirit, till it returns to God who gave it. And, in numberless instances, it comes short of doing the will of God, as Adam did in paradise. Hence the best of men may say from the heart,

'Every moment, Lord, I need The merit of thy death',

for innumerable violations of the Adamic as well as the angelic law. It is well, therefore, for us, that we are not now under these, but under the law of love.'[75]

Elsewhere in his published writings Wesley had already elaborated on the various aspects of human fallibility summarized in that passage from his mature sermon 'On Perfection'. In his earlier discourse on 'Christian Perfection', which was specifically designed to clarify his teaching since it had been the butt of criticism, Wesley began his series of negations by maintaining that Christians are not perfect in knowledge.[76] Sanctification does not bring freedom from ignorance. Even the enlightened believer cannot probe the depths of God's being or understand the inter-personal relationships of the Holy Trinity. He is incapable of grasping the mystery of the incarnation or pinpointing the times and seasons in the calendar of eschatology. At a more practical level, he is unaware of God's providential dispositions and hence must necessarily walk by faith and not by sight. More seriously, this imperfection of knowledge may also lead man into unconscious transgressions which, though they constitute an infringement of God's law, cannot be said to violate the higher law of love since the intention is absent.[77]

Ignorance may also lead to mistakes: indeed they are an almost inevitable consequence of it. If we only 'know in part' then we are liable to err in proportion to our deficiency. Wesley had no hesitation in asserting that 'the children of God do not mistake as to the things essential to salvation', but in peripheral matters relating to facts and circumstances they may very easily do so.[78] Even in the interpretation of Scripture, no human judgement is infallible.[79] 'While we breathe, we shall more or less mistake', Wesley told Dorothy Furly. 'If therefore Christian perfection implies this, we must not expect it till after death.'[80] Nor does sanctification guarantee freedom from infirmities. But Wesley was careful to define what he meant. 'Let us not give that soft title to known sins, as the manner of some is,' he warned. 'I mean hereby not only those which are properly termed bodily infirmities, but all those inward or outward imperfections which are not of a moral nature'.[81] He went on to instance mental confusion, forgetfulness, slowness of speech and the like.

Nor can Christians expect to be completely free from temptation on this side of the grave.[82] The Son of God himself was subject to the assaults of the evil one and his followers will not escape. In explaining his position in a letter to Bishop Gibson, Wesley expressed the view that 'there is no such perfection in this life as implies an entire deliverance from manifold temptations'.[83] Some may enjoy a temporary respite but Satan will doubtless return at an early opportunity.

Wesley went out of his way to make it clear that sanctification is *not unimprovable*. There is no perfection 'which does not admit of a continual increase'. [84] The believer never arrives. He is always going on to maturity. He is being perfected as well as made perfect. 'How much soever any man has attained, or in how high a degree soever he is perfect, he hath still need to 'grow in grace', and daily to advance in the knowledge and love of God his Saviour'.[85] This recognition of the need for continual growth is a key factor in Wesley's doctrine of sanctification, as we shall shortly see when we come to review his positive insights. Perfection is never a state that has been attained: it is always a condition that is being maintained and which is capable of improvement to the very end. In meeting objections raised by his detractors, Wesley repeatedly found it necessary to defend himself against the calumny that he taught a perfection that passed beyond any further reliance on the sacrifice of the Cross. He countered such misrepresentations by arguing that sanctification is not independent of the atonement but sustained by it. 'A perfection that perfectly fulfils the whole law and so needs not the merits of Christ? I acknowledge none such - I do now and always did protest against it.'[86] In his *Thoughts on Christian Perfection* Wesley raised the question as to whether sanctification does not 'exclude the necessity of a Mediator?'[87] Is not the priestly office of Christ rendered superfluous? Here is the emphatic answer: 'Far from it. None feel their need of Christ like these; none so entirely depend on him. For Christ does not give life to the soul separate from, but in and with himself.'[88] In his *Farther Thoughts on Christian Perfection* Wesley confirmed this insistence. 'The holiest of men still need Christ, as their Prophet, as 'the light of the world'. For he does not give them light, but from moment to moment. The instant he withdraws all is darkness. They still need Christ as their King, for God does not give them a stock of holiness. But unless they receive a supply every moment, nothing but unholiness would remain. They still need Christ as their Priest, to make atonement for their holy things. Even perfect holiness is acceptable to God only through Jesus Christ.'[89]

In accordance with his existential understanding of sanctification, as maintained in a moment by moment experience, Wesley believed that it was *not irreversible*. It could be lost. At first he was inclined to believe that no-one who had entered into the grace of sanctification could conceivably fall away from it. It was his brother Charles who persuaded him that this is not the case. He thereupon agreed to retract certain expressions in the Methodist hymns which implied such an impossibility.[90]

The negative safeguards with which Wesley protected his doctrine of sanctification appear mainly in the context of controversy as he was compelled to defend his position from attack. But his central purpose was positive and we approximate more closely to Wesley's statement of his teaching as we listen to his affirmations rather than to his denials. Our concern in this closing enquiry is less with his reiteration of accepted principles within the tradition of biblical orthodoxy than with some distinctive insights which have helped to shape the theological understanding of sanctification since his day.

3. We have seen that Wesley correctly envisaged sanctification as related to and consequent on justification. 'At the same time that we are justified, yea, in that very moment, sanctification begins,' he declared in his seminal sermon on 'The Scripture Way of Salvation'. 'In that instant we are born again, born from above, born of the Spirit: there is a *real* as well as a *relative* change'.[91] For Wesley the positional righteousness made possible in the moment of justification must immediately be accompanied by a progressive, actual righteousness reflected in conduct and character. Otherwise the grace of God is received in vain.[92] Wesley saw with exceptional clarity that sanctification is the purpose of justification. It is not a mere appendage or an accidental consequence. The reason why a man is put right with God is that he should live righteously.

Wesley did not, however, fall into the trap of identifying sanctification with justification, as did the Moravians and Quakers.[93] Though sanctification is 'in some degree, the immediate fruit of justification', it is also 'a distinct gift of God and of a totally different nature'.[94]   Whereas justification may be defined as 'what God does for us through his Son', sanctification is 'what he works in us by his Spirit'.[95]   The distinction lies in the fact that sanctification has to do with the ongoing life of the Christian, while justification is primarily a matter of initial status.   Hence, for Wesley, sanctification is more properly linked with the new birth in which this life begins.[96]

Wesley's emphasis on a righteousness that is not only imputed but actually imparted and implanted came under fire from some of his theological opponents. He was accused both by the hyper-Calvinists and by members of the Moravian fraternity (including Count Zinzendorf himself) of preaching 'inherent righteousness' instead of 'God's righteousness'.[97]   Concern to safeguard the Reformation principle of sovereign grace led to an insistence that the sanctity of the Christian is not something which inheres in or actually belongs to him, but, as in justification, is no more than the objective righteousness of Christ credited to the believer. Wesley replied that scriptural holiness is the image of God restored in man, as Christ dwells in his heart by faith. 'Every believer has holiness in, though not from, himself.'[98] It is not his product or possession: it is not a righteousness of his own, but the righteousness of Christ.   Yet it is made effective through his inner disposition rather than superimposed upon his personality. Scriptural holiness is intrinsic while still divine.   In a perceptive discussion of these important issues, Donal J. Dorr concludes: 'Wesley has carefully placed himself between the two extremes - the extreme of a merely imputed holiness, and the extreme of a holiness so inherent that it is possessed independently of God'.[99]

'By faith we are saved from sin, and made holy,' announced Wesley in a sermon dated as late as 1790, claiming that this is what he had preached for fifty years.[100]   But this does not mean that the law loses its force or that obedience is no longer required. As Rupert Davies reminds us, 'the longest and fiercest battle that Wesley had to fight - and he fought it with tenacity and courage - was against those who maintained that once a man was justified by faith he was exempt from keeping God's commandments; he was above such elementary things, he was on the verge of perfection or actually in the enjoyment of it'.[101] 'The imagination, that faith *supersedes* holiness, is the marrow of Antinomianism', Wesley trenchantly maintained in the sermon quoted above.[102] But having demonstrated that, so far from bypassing holiness, faith is intended to produce it, Wesley could hardly lay too much stress on the place of faith in sanctification. 'That great truth, 'that we are saved by faith,' will never be worn out: and that sanctifying as well as justifying faith is the free gift of God'.[103] In other words, he set his doctrine within the Protestant framework of justification by faith, not within the then current Roman framework of justification by faith and works.[104] As Robert Monk has shown, Wesley was not only in line with the Reformation but also an heir of the Puritans.[105] 'For Wesley', declares Professor Albert Outler, 'the doctrine of perfection was yet another way of celebrating the *sovereignty* of grace!'[106]

Wesley's doctrine of sanctification, as we have seen, expressed the optimism of grace with regard to the believer's deliverance from sin. This means deliverance from inward as well as outward sin.[107] 'The whole tenor of Scripture declares Christ came to 'destroy the works of the devil, to save us from our sins' - all the works of the devil, all our sins, without any exception or limitation'.[108] The glorious privilege of every Christian is to be 'so far perfect as not to commit sin'.[109] He is delivered from its guilt and power, though not from its being.[110] That is to say, 'a man may have the Spirit of God dwelling in him, and may "walk after the Spirit", though he still feels "the flesh lusting against the Spirit"'.[111] Whether sin is suspended or extinguished Wesley refused to dispute.[112] He told Joseph Benson that he used the word 'destroyed' because Paul does: 'suspended' he could not find in his Bible.[113] He preferred to regard sin as excluded or expelled by love. It was a matter of displacement. Love and sin cannot live together. There is no room for both.

All this brings us to what Wesley dubbed 'the scarecrow of sinless perfection'.[114] There is an apparent inconsistency in his attitude to the charges that were brought against him on this score. On the one hand we hear him refusing to contend for it, since the term is not scriptural, and claiming that it is a phrase he never uses lest he should seem to contradict himself.[115] But on the other hand he tells his brother Charles that though he did not contend for it neither did he object to it.[116] In his reply to Edmund Gibson he said that he might plead 'not guilty' since one ingredient in the Bishop's account of what the Methodists were alleged to preach was 'freedom from temptation'.[117] But Wesley did not decline the charge. Instead he treated his episcopal correspondent to what he called his 'coolest thoughts upon this head' in an extract from the preface to the volume of hymns published in 1742.[118] Now it is obvious that Wesley never countenanced any interpretation of sinless perfection which jeopardized the uniqueness of Christ or hinted that it is possible for the Christian to arrive at a state of sinlessness which pre-empts the future. Wesley's outlook was existential. His was the theology of the present moment. In this moment the believer may be free from sin. That does not guarantee even the next moment. But at least this moment may be sinless; and from the angle of God's enabling grace, if this moment, why not the next and indeed every moment? Wesley was reluctant to repudiate the term lest he should appear to circumscribe the scope of grace. The alternative to sinless perfection was sinful perfection - a blasphemous contradiction in terms which lay at the heart of antinomianism.

In encouraging John Fletcher to press on with the preparation of a volume containing six dialogues on cardinal Christian doctrines, Wesley referred to Christian perfection as a 'a continued miracle'.[119] He compared it with the force of gravity. Whatever Wesley also taught about an instantaneous work of grace in the believer must be assessed in the context of this gradual growth. Though he did not employ the precise language of the following century, he anticipated the exponents of the early Keswick Convention message in recognizing a crisis within the process.[120] But his primary preoccupation was with the latter. 'Go on, in your own way, what God has peculiarly called you to', he urged his brother Charles. 'Press the *instantaneous* blessing: then I shall have more time for my peculiar calling, enforcing the *gradual* work'.[121] The verbs in his description of the Christian's life are all in the present continuous tense. 'God is continually breathing, as it were, upon the soul, and his soul is breathing into God. Grace is descending into his heart; and prayer and praise ascending to heaven; and by this intercourse between God and man, this fellowship with the Father and the Son, as by a kind of spiritual respiration, the life of God in the soul is sustained; and the child of God grows up, till he comes to the "full measure of the stature of Christ"'.[122] Elsewhere Wesley speaks about the continual inspiration of the Spirit filling the heart with love like a well of water springing up into everlasting life.[123]

'Moment by moment' was a principle with Wesley long before it was adopted by the holiness movements of the later nineteenth century. It is only by sheer grace that believers can overcome sin, he argued. 'Nor is it given all at once, as if they had a stock laid up for many years; but from moment to moment.'[124] And again: 'By faith we feel the power of Christ every moment resting upon us, whereby alone we are what we are; whereby we are enabled to continue in spiritual life, and without which, notwithstanding all our present holiness, we should be devils the next moment'.[125]

It was in the context of this constantly maintained condition that Wesley found a place for an instantaneous experience. It marked a transition to entire sanctification. It did not interrupt the process of growth but gave it a fresh impetus and lifted it to a new level. Since such entire sanctification takes place in response to faith and amounts to a powerful act of intervention by God himself, it is regarded as the work of a moment.[126] 'If you seek it by faith, you may expect it *as you are*; and if as you are, then expect it *now*. It is of importance to observe, that there is an inseparable connection between these three points - expect it by *faith*; expect it *as you are*; and expect it *now*. To deny one of them is to deny them all; to allow one is to allow them all'.[127] This crisis aspect of sanctification Wesley called 'a second change', 'a farther change', 'a blessed change', 'the instantaneous blessing', 'the second awakening', 'a second work of grace', 'a second blessing', or 'the second blessing'.[128]

Wesley recognized quite candidly that the Scriptures are not explicit as to whether the instantaneous work is essential. 'The point is not determined, at least not in express terms, in any part of the oracles of God. Every man therefore may abound in his own sense, provided he will allow the same liberty to his neighbour; provided he will not be angry at those who differ from his opinion, nor entertain hard thoughts concerning them. Permit me likewise to add one thing more. Be the change instantaneous or gradual, see that you never rest till it is wrought in your own soul, if you desire to dwell with God in glory'.[129] With that characteristically personal and pointed appeal we may appropriately conclude this review of Wesley's positive insights.

Our survey has sought to clarify John Wesley's teaching on sanctification and to underline its continuing relevance. It has confirmed the conclusions reached by Professor Gerald R. Cragg in his treatment of *Reason and Authority in the Eighteenth Century*. He points out that Wesley 'believed that perfection was the natural consequence of the total process of salvation, and he saw it as God's special gift to the Methodist people.'[130] At the same time it was far from easy to interpret and apply. In his attempt to do so Wesley was not always absolutely consistent. 'But the problems inherent in perfection could not be regarded as sufficient grounds for neglecting it,' Cragg adds, 'and to the end Wesley insisted that it be given its proper place in the life of his societies. This, indeed, is the most constant strain in his thought.'[131]

REFERENCES

1. *John Wesley: An Autobiographical Sketch of the Man and his Thought*, ed. Ole E. Borgen, Leiden, E.J. Brill, 1966, p.xiii.
2. William R. Cannon, 'Perfection', *The London Quarterly and Holborn Review* (LQR), July 1959, p.213.
3. *The Works of the Rev. John Wesley*, 3rd edition, ed. Thomas Jackson, London, John Mason, 14 vols. 1829-31 (*Works*) 8.472.
4. *The Letters of the Rev. John Wesley*, Standard Edition, ed. John Telford, London, Epworth Press, 8 vols, 1931 (*Letters*), 4.237.
5. Cf. E. Gordon Rupp, 'The Future of the Methodist Tradition', LQR, July 1959, p.267.
6. *Works*, 6. 416.
7. Franz Hildebrandt, 'Can the Distinctive Methodist Emphasis be said to be Rooted in the New Testament?', LQR, July 1959, p.233. George Croft Cell, in *The Rediscovery of John Wesley*, New York, Henry Holt, 1935, p.347, insists that Wesley's doctrine of holiness 'is not.... a provincialism of the Wesleyan Reformation.... but must rather be understood and appreciated in the widest perspective of the whole prophetic Christian movement.'
8. *Letters*, 5.315.
9. *Works*, 8.290.
10. *Letters*, 5.290.
11. *Works*, 8.47.
12. *Ibid.*
13. Harald Lindström, *Wesley and Sanctification: A Study in the Doctrine of Salvation*, Stockholm, Nya Bokforlags, 1946, p.123.
14. For Middleton, see Roland N. Strömberg, *Religious Liberalism in Eighteenth Century England*, Oxford, Oxford University Press, 1954, pp. 75-8.
15. *Letters*, 2.375.
16. Cell, *op. cit.*, p.11.
17. Adolf Harnack, *What is Christianity? Sixteen Lectures*, E.T. London, Williams and Norgate, 1901.
18. *Works*, 11.384. Wesley included the entire preface in *A Plain Account of Christian Perfection*.
19. *Letters*, 5.208
20. *Works*, 8.109
21. *The Journal of the Rev. John Wesley*, Standard Edition, ed. Nehemiah Curnock, London, Epworth Press, 8 vols, 1909-16 (*Journal*), 2.275.
22. Henry Scougal, *The Life of God in the Soul of Man*: or the *Nature and Excellency of the Christian Religion* .... London, Downing, 1677. For a useful digest and evaluation of Scougal's book, see Martin Schmidt, *John Wesley: A Theological Biography*, London, Epworth Press, E.T. 1962, Vol. I, pp.53-7. Wesley himself published a shortened version in 1770. For Susanna Wesley's estimate of Scougal, see her probable letter to John on October 25th 1732, reproduced in *Proceedings of the Wesley Historical Society*, 18.169-72. F.F. Bretherton took the view that Susanna was transcribing a letter from her husband Samuel (*ibid.*, 172).
23. Luke Tyerman, *The Life of the Rev. George Whitefield*, London, Hodder and Stoughton, 1890. Vol. I, p.17.
24. *Works*, 6.414.
25. *Ibid.*
26. *Works*, 11.451; cf. *Letters*, 3.168. William Dodd (1729-1777), an Anglican clergyman, held two lectureships in West Ham and St. Olave's, Hart Street. He was a highly popular preacher who was later executed for forgery. Wesley visited him in prison.
27. *Works*, 6.414.
28. *Works*, 8.19.
29. *Ibid.*
30. *Ibid.*, 182
31. *Works*, 11.384
32. *Ibid.*
33. *The Standard Sermons of John Wesley*, ed. Edward H. Sugden, London, Epworth Press, 1921 (*Sermons*), 2.223-4.

34. *Letters*, 5.203
36. *Ibid.*
38. *Ibid.*
40. *Ibid.*
42. *Letters*, 7.129; cf. *Works*, 8.344.
44. 'Man's chief end is to glorify God, and to enjoy him for ever.' *The Confession of Faith. The Larger and Shorter Catechism*, ed. W. Grant, Inverness, Free Church of Scotland, 1958, p.287.
45. *Works*, 8.65.
47. *Ibid.*
49. *Letters*, 5.6.
51. *Letters*, 6.266.
53. *Letters*, 4.216.
55. *Letters*, 5.223.
57. *Letters*, 3.167.
59. *Letters*, 4.212.
61. *Works*, 8.21-2
63. *Letters*, 5.20.
65. *Sermons*, 2.151.
67. *Letters*, 8.272.
69. *Ibid.*, 269.
71. *Works*, 6.412.
73. *Ibid.*
75. *Works*, 6.412-3.
77. *Letters*, 4.191.
79. *Ibid.*, 154.
81. *Sermons*, 2.155.
83. *Letters*, 2.280.
85. *Sermons*, 2.156.
87. *Works*, 11.395.
89. *Ibid.*, 417.
91. *Sermons*, 2.446.

35. *Sermons*, 2.56-7.
37. *Works*, 6.413.
39. *Works*, 8.107.
41. *Works*, 7.297.
43. *Sermons*, 1.474.

46. *Ibid.*
48. *Works*. 6.488.
50. *Ibid.*
52. *Letters*, 7.120.
54. *Sermons*, 2.448.
56. *Letters*, 4.192.
58. *Ibid.*, 168.
60. *Ibid.*, 190.
62. *Letters*, 4.188.
64. *Letters*, 3.168.
66. *Letters*, 4.216.
68. *Letters*, 4.208.
70. *Ibid.*, 213.
72. *Ibid.*
74. Lindström, *op. cit.*, pp. 153-4.
76. *Sermons*, s.152; cf. *Works*, 11.374.
78. *Sermons*, 2.153.
80. *Letters*, 4.188.
82. *Ibid.*; cf. *Letters*, 4.192
84. *Sermons*, 2.156; cf.*Works*, 11.374.
86. *Letters*, 4.213.
88. *Ibid.*
90. *Letters*, 4,187; cf. 5.38-9.

92. *Letters*, 5.81-2.'I apprehend nothing would be more likely to hurt the soul than undervaluing the grace already received.'
93. Wesley repudiated the Moravian conflation of justification and sanctification which taught 'that we are sanctified wholly the moment we are justified, and are neither more nor less holy to the day of our death; entire sanctification, and entire justification, being in one and the same instant' (*Works*, 10.202). When Thomas Whitehead enquired whether there was any difference between Quakerism and Christianity, Wesley replied that the major issue at stake was justification by faith. Quaker teaching he took to be 'flat justification by works.' 'The ground of his mistake,' Wesley continued, 'is the not understanding the meaning of the word "justification". For Robert Barclay takes it in the same sense as the Papists do, confounding it with sanctification. So in page 208 of his *Apology*, he says in express terms, 'Justification, taken in its proper signification, is making one just, and is all one with sanctification.' (*Letters*, 2.118).
94. *Sermons*, 1.119.
95. *Ibid.*
96. *Ibid.*, 299-300; cf. *Letters*, 4.67, where the new birth is described as 'the beginning of sanctification.'
97. *Works*, 10.277.
98. *Ibid.*, 203.
99. Donal J. Dorr, 'Wesley's Teaching on the Nature of Holiness', LQR, July 1965, p.236.
100. *Works*, 7.317.
101. Rupert E. Davies, 'The People Called Methodists. 1. Our Doctrines', in *A History of the Methodist Church in Great Britain*, ed. Rupert E. Davies and E. Gordon Rupp, London. Epworth Press, Vol. I, 1965, p.167.
102. *Works*, 7.317.
103. *Letters*, 4.268.

104. Colin W. Williams, *John Wesley's Theology Today*, London, Epworth Press, 1960, p.175.
105. Robert C. Monk, *John Wesley: His Puritan Heritage. A Study of the Christian Life*, New York, Abingdon Press, 1966, p.68.
106. *John Wesley*, ed. Albert C. Outler, New York, Oxford University Press, 1964, p.253.
107. *Letters*, 2.213. 'It undoubtedly implies salvation from all sin, inward and outward, into all holiness.'
108. *Letters*, 4.12.
109. *Sermons*, 2.169; cf. *Works*, 11.376.
110. *Sermons*, 2.373.　　　　111. *Ibid.*, 373-4.
112. *Letters*, 4.213.　　　　113. *Letters*, 5.204.
114. *Letters*, 2.229; *Works*, 8.432.　　115. *Letters*, 4.213.
116. *Ibid.*, 187; cf *Letters*, 5.39.
117. *Letters*, 2.280.　　　　118. *Ibid.*
119. *Letters*, 5.4.　　　　120. *Letters*, 3.213; 4.187; 5.39, 210.
121. *Letters*, 5.16.
122. *Sermons*, 2.234; cf. John Wesley, *Explanatory Notes upon the New Testament*, London, Epworth Press, 1929 (1754), p.911 on I John 3:9. '*Whosoever is born of God* - by living faith, whereby God is continually breathing spiritual life into his soul, and his soul is continually breathing out love and prayer to God, *doth not commit sin.*'
123. Cf. *Works*, 8.80, 107; 12.77.　　124. *Sermons*, 2.389.
125. *Ibid.*, 393.　　　　126. *Letters*, 4.192.
127. *Sermons*, 2.460.
128. *Letters*, 5.215, *Sermons*, 2.391; *Ibid.*, 395; *Works*, 8.329; *Letters*, 5.16; *Letters*, 6.144-5; *Letters*, 4.133; *Letters*, 3.212, 5.315; *Letters*, 6.116.
129. *Works*, 6.490.
130. Gerald R. Cragg, *Reason and Authority in the Eighteenth Century*, Cambridge, Cambridge Univ. Press, 1964, pp.168-9.
131. *Ibid.*, p.169.

EXPLANATORY NOTES

Supralapsarianism. (p. 52) *The view that human destiny has already been determined before the fall.*

Posting. (p. 57) *An archaism meaning 'hastening', lit. 'to travel by post-horse'.*

LUTHER'S PRINCIPLES OF
BIBLICAL INTERPRETATION
by Dr Skevington Wood

'Protestant interpretation of the Bible', according to Professor Robert M. Grant of Chicago, 'owes its life to the spirit of the Reformation.'[1]   And after making that statement, Dr. Grant proceeds to cite a definitive affirmation of Martin Luther at the Leipzig Debate as reflecting the revolutionary new attitude. 'No believing Christian can be forced to recognise any authority beyond the sacred Scripture, which is exclusively invested with Divine right.'[2]   Over against the pretentious claims of the papacy, Luther set the Word of God as its own interpreter, through the operation of the Holy Spirit, independent of Church and councils, of fathers and tradition. Thus opened a fresh and significant chapter in the history of hermeneutics.

The Bible, of course, was central in the reforming policy of Luther. 'As a theologian,' wrote Professor Henry E. Jacobs, 'Luther's chief effort, on the negative side, was to free theology from its bondage to philosophy, and to return to the simplicity of Scripture. He was dissatisfied with technical theological terms because of their inadequacy, even when the elements of truth they contained restrained him from abandoning them. He was not without a historical sense and reverence for antiquity, provided it was subjected to the tests of Holy Scripture. Scripture was not to be interpreted by the Fathers, but the Fathers were judged by their agreement or disagreement with Scripture.'[3]

I

Interpretation, then, was a focal issue in the Protestant Reformation. That is apparent in Luther's historic confession at the Diet of Worms in 1520, when Johann von Eck, Official General of the Archbishop of Trier, required a recantation of his alleged errors. 'Unless I am convinced by the testimonies of the Holy Scripture or evident reason (for I believe neither in the Pope nor Councils alone, since it has been established that they have often erred and contradicted themselves), I am bound by the Scriptures adduced by me and my conscience has been taken captive by the Word of God, and I am neither able nor willing to recant, since it is neither safe nor right to act against conscience. God help me. Amen.'[4]   The earliest printed version inserted the now famous declaration, 'Here I stand, I cannot do otherwise.'

Roland Bainton thinks that the words, though not actually recorded on the spot, could yet be genuine because the listeners may have been too moved at the moment to write them down.[5] Or perhaps they were drowned in the ensuing commotion, for Conrad Peutinger reports: 'There was a great noise.'[6] In any case, they symbolize Luther's position. He took his stand upon the sole authority of Scripture and repudiated all other interpretations of it save its own.

The centrality of interpretation in the Reformation issue is even more markedly apparent in Luther's interview with Cardinal Cajetan at Augsburg in 1518. In the estimate of Professor Jedin of Bonn, Cajetan was the greatest theologian of his time, held in the highest esteem for his erudite commentary on the *Summa Theologica* of Thomas Aquinas, from whom he had taken his monastic name as a Dominican.[7] No doubt he imagined that he would have little difficulty in convincing the youthful rebel from Wittenberg that his views were doctrinally untenable. He therefore demanded an unequivocal recantation. But this Luther's conscience would not allow him to make unless he was first informed and then convinced of his errors from the Word of God, untrammelled by any superimposed interpretation. When he refused to withdraw his previous denial of the validity of indulgences, Cajetan quoted the *Extravagante* of Clement VI's Papal Bull *Unigenitus* of 1343, which plainly asserted that Christ's passion and death had acquired an inexhaustible treasure for the Church, reserved in heaven, to which the Virgin Mary and the saints continued to contribute and which had been specifically entrusted to Peter and his successors for the purpose of releasing the faithful from their temporal penalties. But the Cardinal discovered that Luther was more conversant with Canon Law than he had assumed and was, indeed, prepared to press a legal quibble about the verb *acquisivit*.

Moreover, as Schwiebert points out, 'in raising the question of the true treasure of the Church, the Gospel, Cajetan had touched the very heart of Luther's new theology, the doctrine of justification by faith alone. Luther had no intentions of being refuted on the evidence of a papal bull when his whole teaching had been painfully rediscovered on the basis of the New Testament. With Luther this was a matter so vital that he would die rather than deny his new understanding of Scripture unless convinced of error.'[8] And so he bluntly rejected the authority of the decretal together with that of the Pope who promulgated it, on the sole ground that it misrepresented Scripture. Luther's

Nominalist training at Erfurt may have laid the foundations of his attitude, for William of Ockham had affirmed that 'Holy Scriptures cannot err, the Pope can'.[9] In the written statement submitted to Cajetan on the third day of the enquiry Luther explained his position more fully. 'Indeed I did not possess the extraordinary indiscretion so as to discard so many important clear proofs of Scripture on account of a single ambiguous and obscure decretal of a Pope who is a mere human being. Much rather I considered it proper that the words of Scripture, in which saints are described as being deficient in merits, are to be preferred to human words in which the saints are said to have more merits than they need. For a Pope is not above but under the Word of God.'[10] The Cardinal, however, reminded Luther that Scripture itself has to be interpreted and that the Pope is the supreme interpreter. His ruling takes precedence over Church, Council or even Scripture itself. 'His Holiness abuses Scripture', retorted Luther. 'I deny that he is above Scripture.' Although Cajetan swore that Luther must leave the court and not return unless he was prepared to retract, he nevertheless confided afterwards to Staupitz: 'I am not going to talk with him any more. His eyes are as deep as a lake, and there are amazing speculations in his head.'[11] Clearly, the nub of Luther's argument lay in his challenge to the Roman monopoly of interpretation. As Harnack put the situation: 'If a tradition, a text of Scripture or a dogmatic affirmation was inconvenient, the Church, that is Rome, had the right of interpreting.'[12] In his treatise *The Papacy at Rome* - an answer to Eck's notorious *Thirteenth Thesis* - Luther complained that the papists interpreted the Scriptures in accordance with their own insane folly and that the Pope 'soiled them like a snivelling child'.[13] 'Thus we can see how beautifully the Romanists treat the Scriptures and make out of them what they like, as if they were a nose of wax to be pulled around at will.'[14] And again later,in his defence of the articles condemned in the Bull of 1520: 'Lo, thus the Pope tricks and seduces the whole world; he takes out of the Divine Word what he will, though it belongs equally to everybody, and pretends to drink malmsey out of the same cask from which others can scarcely get water. God's simple, single Word, with its one single virtue, is gold for him, but he will not let others pass it as copper. Cease, Pope; the game has gone far enough.'[15]

But even as early as 1517, when Luther nailed his Ninety-Five Theses to the church door at Wittenberg in order to initiate an academic disputation on indulgences, interpretation is seen to be the underlying issue. That classic document opens with this pronouncement: 'Our Lord and Master Jesus Christ, when he said *Poenitentiam agite* willed that the whole life of believers should be repentance.'[16] Luther proceeds to discuss the interpretation of Matthew iv. 17 and the Vulgate rendering 'Do penance' for the Greek *metanoeite*. 'This word cannot be understood to mean sacramental penance i.e. confession and satisfaction, which is administered by the priests. Yet it means not inward repentance only; nay, there is no inward repentance which does not outwardly work divers mortifications of the flesh. The penalty (of sin), therefore, continues so long as hatred of self continues; for this is the true inward repentance, and continues until our entrance into the Kingdom of heaven.'[17] Although the Theses, as Jacobs rightly adjudges, can scarcely be called in their entirety 'a trumpet-blast of reform',[18] and Luther was still in the process of emancipation from Rome, nevertheless it is of the utmost significance that at the outset he should seek to lay a foundation of sound exegesis.

Interpretation, then, was a fundamental issue in the Reformation controversy. Luther's awareness of its cruciality and his ability to apply it to the situation which confronted him arose from his own religious experience. Interpretation was a key concern in his individual struggle for spiritual existence before he made it so in the collective conflict with Rome. To this we must turn, for, as Professor Warren A. Quanbeck informs us in a recent and helpful essay, 'in order to understand Luther's principles of interpretation, it is necessary to set forth the inner development which was instrumental in forming them.'[19] Luther, like Wesley after him, was *homo unius libri. Sola Scriptura* was not only the battle-cry of a crusade: it was the pole-star of his own heart and mind. 'All that Luther was as a Christian man', wrote Dr. Stork, 'he owed to the Bible; and all that he did as a Reformer he achieved through the instrumentality of the Divine Word. From the time he found Christ, the Bible was to him the inspiration, the beauty and joy of his life. It was his guide in every perplexity; his solace in every sorrow and his watch-word in every battle for the truth.'[20]

We need not traverse again at any length the now reasonably familiar ground of Luther's rediscovery of the Bible in his personal experience. Suffice to say that the Protestant Reformation really started not on the steps of the Scala Sancta in Rome (where pious legend may have overlaid the tale) nor at the entrance to the newly built Schlosskirche at Wittenberg (where the Theses were intended to inaugurate a discussion rather than touch off a revolt), but in the tower room of the Augustinian cloister where Luther sat before an open Bible and allowed Almighty God to address him face to face. This *Türmerlebnis* ('tower discovery') is dated by Schwiebert as 'some time in the fall of 1514'.[21] It represents the final explosion in a chain reaction which began with Luther's first introduction to the Latin Bible, probably in the Cathedral at Magdeburg.[22]

The real significance of the tower discovery lies in the realm of interpretation. Luther's hand at last grasped the key with which the Scriptures could be unlocked. He has left an autobiographical account in the preface to the Latin edition of his works published in 1545. He tells us that as he searched the Word of God he was led to devote particular attention to the Epistle to the Romans . The expression *iustitia Dei* in i.17 was a considerable stumbling-block to him since his scholastic conditioning inclined him to assume that it referred to God's punitive justice . 'The concept of "God's righteousness" was repulsive to me, as I was accustomed to interpret it according to scholastic philosophy, namely, as the "formal or active" righteousness in which God proves Himself righteous in that He punishes the sinner as an unrighteous person... until after days and nights of wrestling with the problem, God finally took pity on me, so that I was able to comprehend the inner connection between the two expressions "the righteousness of God revealed in the Gospel" and "the just shall live by faith". Then I began to comprehend "the righteousness of God" through faith; that the "righteousness of God" which is revealed through the Gospel was to be understood in a passive sense in which God through mercy justifies man by faith, as it is written "the just shall live by faith". Now I felt exactly as though I had been born again, and I believed that I had entered Paradise through widely opened doors. I then went through the Holy Scriptures as far as I could recall them from memory, and I found in other parts the same sense: the "work of God" is that which He works in us, the "strength of God" is that through which He makes us strong, the "wisdom of God" is that through which He makes us wise, and so the power of God, the blessing of God and the honour of God are likewise to be interpreted. As violently as I had formerly hated the expression "righteousness of God", so I was now as violently compelled to embrace the new conception of grace, and thus, for me, the expression really opened the gates of Paradise.'[23]

This experience marked the beginning of Luther's attachment to justification by faith as the plumbline by which he tested every theological opinion. But it was cradled in Scripture and was the fruit of his new interpretative insight. Luther's 'illumination', as he calls it in his *Table Talk*, or his 'inspiration', as Schwarz prefers to denominate it,[24] transformed the whole Bible for him and supplied his over-all hermeneutical clue. He had grasped the significance of one centripetal portion of God's Word: by it he proceeded to reinterpret the rest. As Schwarz has elucidated it, 'The meaning of one passage had been revealed to him. He therefore had received the true understanding of this one verse. Holy Writ, being God's revelation, must of necessity be a unity and its contents be in agreement. It is therefore permissible, or even necessary, to interpret the Bible in accordance with Romans i:17, if the true meaning of this verse has been revealed.'[25] Luther's entire exegetical output stems from this comprehension which he recognizes as a gift from God. 'I have not dared nor am I able to boast of anything but the Word of truth which the Lord has given me.'[26] Elsewhere he speaks of Christ, 'Who is the Master of my doctrine and also will witness on the Last Day that this doctrine is not mine but His own pure Gospel'.[27] And writing to Kurfurst Friedrich in 1522 he claims that he has not received the gospel from man, 'but solely from heaven through our Lord Jesus Christ'.[28]

II

The foregoing historical exposition has been necessary to demonstrate the pivotal importance of interpretation both in the testimony of Protestantism and the personal experience of Luther himself. It has served to indicate that Luther's reappraisal dates from the earliest period of his career as an exegete and that in the many direct citations which will follow in this lecture (for we are anxious to let Luther speak for himself) we need not draw any overemphasized distinction between the younger and the more mature reformer. After the decisive moment of the *Türmerlebnis* there was development, to be sure, though not serious divergence. As Prenter says in *Spiritus Creator*, 'the development is within the new evangelical view of life and not away from it. It is development, therefore, which does not signify any modification of the basic view, but is rather a progressive and final struggle with the traditional views based on the unchanged fundamental conclusion.'[29] With this reassurance, we may go on to examine the works of Luther in their widest range with a view to laying bare his leading hermeneutical principles.

It is too often supposed that Luther's exegetical achievement was virtually negligible. A contributor to a well-known encyclopaedia of a former generation could even affirm that 'of the Reformers Luther did little strictly exegetical work apart from his preaching'.[30] That is wide of the mark on two counts. In the first place, the list of Luther's 'strictly exegetical work' is sufficiently impressive in itself. When in the year 1512 he accepted the chair of Biblical Studies in the University of Wittenberg he was virtually committing himself to the task of exposition as a life work. He was not slack concerning the promise implicit in his vocation. For the remainder of his career he delivered at least two or three lectures each week, unless prevented by sickness or his multifarious activities in the cause of the Reformation. The complete catalogue is as under.

1513 - 1514	Psalms	1526	Ecclesiastes
1515 - 1516	Romans	1527	1 John
1516 - 1517	Galatians	1528	1 Timothy
1517 - 1518	Hebrews	1528 - 1530	Isaiah
1518 - 1521	Psalms: Galatians (revised), Titus, Judges (?)	1530 - 1531	Song of Solomon
		1531 - 1535	Galatians
		1532 - 1535	Psalms
1524 - 1525	Deuteronomy	1535 - 1545	Genesis
1524 - 1526	Minor Prophets		

This does not, of course, include Luther's herculean labour of translation. Yet, despite this considerable productivity, springing from more than competent technical equipment, Luther modestly disclaims any title to distinction. After thanking Johann Brenz for a sight of his commentary on Amos, he adds: 'Far be it from me to suggest any alterations, for I cannot set up as a master in the Divine writings. I only wish to be a learner in that school.'[31]

The noticeable omission from the curriculum, of course, is that of the four Gospels. But as Ebeling explains, there was no exclusion on principle.[32] Luther had once announced a series on the *Pericope*, or Gospel passages in the Liturgy, in 1521, but he was prevented from delivering it because of his summons to the Diet of Worms. Moreover the task of instruction was shared by his colleagues, and we know that Melanchthon gave a course on Matthew and John, whilst Dolsch lectured on Luke and a little later Lambert and Agricola. Luther himself handled the Gospels not in the classroom but in the pulpit. This is not to suggest, however, that his treatment is unworthy of consideration as serious exegesis. We need to realize that our accepted modern distinction between preaching and biblical exposition was unrecognized by Luther. His preaching was always expository in nature and his exegetical lectures invariably contained a homiletical element not nowadays associated, for good or ill, with scholarly comment. As Heikinnen makes clear, Luther's exegesis was essentially *kerygmatic*.[33] This realization that biblical theology and biblical proclamation are inter-related was part of Luther's reappraisal of the Word.

In considering Luther's hermeneutics, as indeed his whole theology, we must beware of undue systematization and the attempt to foster on to his teaching a precision which it does not pretend to possess. Unlike Calvin, Luther displayed a genius which was prophetic rather than logical, intuitive rather than analytical, and we shall go astray if we seek to squeeze his contribution into any conventional mould. For him the Bible was not so much a codification of precepts and principles as a living and life-giving message and his own exposition of it is in organic rather than organizational terms. Even if the co-ordinating scheme is undeveloped, the unity of thought is nevertheless real. Nor must we look for unimpeachable consistency throughout Luther's voluminous works. Even Homer nods and there are times when we have to admit that Luther appears to be at odds with himself. This is especially true in the application of his hermeneutical maxims and caused Seeberg to remark, in passing and with a certain delicate restraint, 'that his practice was not always exemplary and devoid of contradiction can merely be hinted at here'.[34] As with these factors in mind we scrutinize Luther's exegetical writings and such other treatises as advert to his methods, what principles of interpretation are seen to emerge?

III

The first has to do with the important matter of presuppositions. These comprise what Professor Martin Scharlemann calls 'the first hermeneutical circle'.[35] He believes that it is quite naïve to suppose that an interpreter can approach the text of Scripture in a totally objective manner, with his mind a *tabula rasa*, so to speak. Any interpreter must needs enter upon his task carrying with him certain presuppositions drawn, if from no superior source, from his own background and experience. Much of our contemporary inability to arrive at a satisfying exegesis of Scripture has arisen either from failure to recognize this phenomenon, or unwillingness to select the right perspective. In theological liberalism, for example, biblical interpretation has been attempted with a method and concepts borrowed from the study of comparative religion, or from the evolutionary assumption. In this way sacred Scripture has been dealt with in a secularized fashion without any genuine endeavour to discover what was the viewpoint of the writers themselves. It is the contribution of Luther, to which we might well allow ourselves to be recalled today, that he insists that the Bible itself must teach us how to interpret the Bible. The first hermeneutical circle is to be drawn from the design of the Word. The sphere from which the methodology of hermeneutics is to be derived is that of Scripture itself. The true principles of biblical interpretation are themselves quarried from biblical sources. To break this circuit is to deprive interpretation of its essential dynamic and authority.

Moreover, the primary presupposition is that which concerns the nature of Scripture. The interpretation of any piece of literature, argues G.H. Schodde, depends upon the character of the work under review. 'Accordingly the rules of the correct interpretation of the Scriptures will depend upon the character of the writings themselves and the principles which an interpreter will employ in his interpretation of the Scriptures will be in harmony with his ideas of what the Scriptures are as to origin, character, history, etc. In the nature of the case the dogmatical stand of the interpreter will materially influence his hermeneutics and exegesis. In the legitimate sense of the term, every interpreter of the Bible is 'prejudiced', i.e. is guided by certain principles which he holds antecedently to his work of interpretation.'[36] Luther was convinced that the nature of Scripture must itself be determined by Scripture. The interpreter must begin by acquiescing to the distinctively biblical conception of the Bible.

Luther leaves us in no doubt as to what this is. 'In Scripture', he writes, 'you are reading not the word of man, but the Word of the most exalted God, Who desires to have disciples that diligently observe and note what He says.'[37] 'It is our unbelief and corrupt carnal mind which does not allow us to perceive and consider that God speaks to us in Scripture, or that Scripture is the Word of God.'[38] 'The entire Scriptures are assigned to the Holy Ghost'; 'the Holy Scriptures did not grow on earth'; 'the Holy Scriptures have been spoken by the Holy Ghost'[39] - these are but a sample from literally hundreds of similar statements which could be adduced.[40] We must not spend time, however, in reaffirming Luther's acceptance of plenary inspiration as an essential presupposition of his exegesis. It is noteworthy that, in an able article in the *Scottish Journal of Theology*, B.A. Gerrish of New York concedes that Luther never really questioned the traditional theory of inerrant Scripture and speaks of his 'strict view of verbal inspiration'.[41]

IV

Moving from the realm of presuppositions to the actual content of Luther's hermeneutical teaching, we shall endeavour to elaborate some of his principles of interpretation arising from the joint watch-words of *sola fide* and *sola Scriptura* - constituting according to Melanchthon the material and formal principles of the Reformation.

James Wood in his recent book on interpretation is surely right in asserting that 'the starting-point for Luther is that Divine inspiration is necessary for the true interpretation of the Bible'.[42] 'If God does not open and explain Holy Writ,' declares Luther, 'none else can understand it; it will remain a closed book, enveloped in darkness.'[43] This, of course, springs from Luther's own experience. It was only when he himself received his inspiration that he was able to grasp the significance of Scripture. He believed that it was necessary to draw on God's grace and wisdom anew for the interpretation of each successive passage. So the primary prerequisite was prayer. 'Therefore the first duty', he told Spalatin, 'is to begin with a prayer of such a nature that God in His great mercy may grant you the true understanding of His words.'[44] Such a prayer is answered when the Holy Spirit interprets the Word which He has already inspired.[45] The instruction of the Spirit is essential to a right division of the Word. 'The Bible cannot be mastered by study or talent', Luther writes again to Spalatin; 'you must rely solely on the influx of the Spirit.'[46] 'No-one can understand God or His Word who has not received such understanding directly from the Holy Ghost.'[47] It is the office of the Spirit to press home the Word, and to ensure its reception. 'For nobody understands His precepts unless it be given him from above.... You understand them, however, because the Holy Spirit teaches you... Therefore those most sadly err who presume to understand the Holy Scriptures and the law of God by taking hold of them with their own understanding and study.'[48] And again, referring to what is recorded in the Fourth Gospel concerning the pre-existent Logos:

'No man can accept it unless his heart has been touched and opened by the Holy Spirit. It is as impossible of comprehension by reason as it is inaccessible to the touch of the hand.'[49]

Such dependence upon the instruction of the Spirit will recognize the limitations of unaided reason. Luther is convinced that it is not within the capacity of the human intellect to understand God's Word. 'Many speculate wisely but nobody is wise in Scripture and understands it if he does not fear the Lord. And he who fears more, understands more. For "the fear of the Lord is the beginning of wisdom".'[50] In one of his letters to an unnamed recipient he satirizes 'these master minds, who love to grovel in God's Word with their human reason, like the sow in a turnip field'.[51] Obviously it is not to be expected that revelational truth should be apprehended by unregenerate reason. 'If it were susceptible to our wisdom', Luther argues, 'then God would not need to reveal it from heaven or proclaim it through Holy Scripture.'[52] So he concludes: 'In it (i.e. the Bible) not one word is of so small account as to allow of our understanding it by reason.'[53] Luther's scepticism concerning the adequacy of reason to arrive at a knowledge of spiritual reality is in part, no doubt, an inheritance from his Ockhamist tutelage.

On the other hand, reason need not be discarded altogether. It is to be subordinated to the Word of God. Luther differentiates between the magisterial and the ministerial uses of reason. 'Our intellect', he says, 'must adjust itself to the Word of God and to Holy Scripture.'[54] Reason in its *usus magisterialis* must not be permitted to intrude upon God's Word. Man's natural knowledge of God, even when it is accurately preserved in his perverted intellect, must nevertheless be subjected to the Word. Otherwise the Word is brought into contempt. But reason in its *usus ministerialis* as 'the receiving subject or apprehending instrument', as Hollaz defines it, must certainly be employed whenever Scripture is referred to as the repository of divine truth.[55] In the words of H.H. Kramm: 'Luther condemns that reason which tries to be wiser than the Word of God, the reason that wants to be an authority criticising the Word of God, or inventing laws and doctrines in addition to the Word of God. This reason is the sign of human pride in unregenerate souls.'[56] It is quite distinct from the submissive reason of the regenerate man which meekly accepts the truths that are revealed in the Book of God. Luther by no means despises learning, but he is only prepared to be guided by such scholarship as is baptized at Pentecost. 'The Holy Spirit teaches man better than all books; He teaches him to understand the Scriptures better than he can understand from the teaching of any other; and of his own accord he does everything God wills he should, so the Law dare make no demands upon him.'[57] 'The captive understanding', comments Quanbeck, 'is Luther's strong expression for the proper relation to the Bible. The exegete is not a free agent, but a prisoner of the Word. He is not at liberty to use Scripture for his own ends, but must bring his life into conformity to its purposes. God does not meet man as an equal, nor put Himself into man's hands to be used like a magician's spook, but retains authority and control.'[58] This existential note recurs throughout Luther's references to the believer's response to the Word. The knowledge to be sought from Scripture is never abstract or esoteric but always related to life as it has to be lived.

Nor is it divorced from personal experience. On the contrary, it is mediated through it. The way in which the Spirit conveys His interpretation of the Word is through the mind and soul of the man who submits himself to the discipline of instruction. In his Introduction to the Magnificat, Luther stresses that in this sacred canticle the Virgin Mary was speaking out of her own experience in which she was enlightened and taught by the Holy Spirit. No-one, he says, can properly apprehend God's Word apart from the Spirit. 'But', he continues, 'no-one can receive it from the Holy Spirit without experiencing, proving and feeling it. In such experience the Holy Spirit instructs us as in His own school, outside of which naught is learned save empty words and idle fables.'[59] Luther anticipated Calvin's emphasis on the testimony of the Spirit by which the Scripture obtains the credit it deserves and commands our unreserved assent.[60] 'No-one is able to speak worthily or to hear any part of Scripture', says Luther, 'if his disposition of mind is not in conformity herewith so that he feel inside what he hears or speaks outside and cries: Yes, indeed that is so!'[61] Hence his maxim: *Sola experientia fecit theologum.* 'Experience is necessary for the understanding of the Word. It is not merely to be repeated and known, but to be lived and felt.'[62] After Luther's death in 1546 a scrap of paper was found on his table containing these words in Latin. 'No-one can understand the Bucolics of Virgil who has not been a herdsman for five years; nor his Georgics unless he has laboured for five years in the fields. In order to understand aright the epistles of Cicero a man must have been full twenty years in the public service of a great State. No-one need fancy he has tasted Holy Scripture who has not ruled the churches for a hundred years with prophets, like Elijah and Elisha, with John the Baptist, Christ and the apostles.'[63]

However, this underscoring of what might be termed experiential interpretation by no means justifies the stale charge of subjectivism raised with such tiresome frequency against Luther. In his generally commendable study, *The Bible in the Church*, Professor Grant appears to fall a victim to this misconception. Luther's subjective spiritual interpretation of Scripture he describes as 'the glory of the Reformation'.[64] By way of contrast, Calvin is represented as a vigorous exponent of a healthier objective type of exegesis. But at the end of the same chapter, after dealing with Calvin, Pascal and the English reformers, Dr Grant returns to Luther. 'The Reformation interpretation of the Bible, as we have seen, was given classical expression by Martin Luther. He rejects the traditional interpretation for it stands in the way of our personal understanding of Scripture. "The teachings of the Fathers are useful only to lead us to the Scriptures, as they were led, and then we must hold to the Scriptures alone."[65] The resulting exegesis is subjective, to be sure; but it is also objective. It is based on the literal meaning of the original writings.... The Bible is not one standard of authority among others, as it was for Medieval Catholicism. It is the sole standard. And it is not an objective standard as it was for Thomas Aquinas. It is a standard at once objective and subjective, for in it and through it God Himself speaks to the human heart. The Bible authenticates itself.'[66] This more balanced summary goes far to correct the impression given earlier by Grant that Luther's approach to the Bible was predominantly subjective. Such, as we have seen, is far from being the case. Luther recognizes the Spirit as the sole Interpreter, but he is also aware that the Spirit must communicate Himself to a receptive medium. His witness is answered by the acquiescing testimony of the regenerate spirit within. Christian experience Luther regarded as itself the product of the biblical message, or, rather, of the power of the Holy Spirit mediated through the Scriptures. 'Thus the congruence of experience and exposition in the study of the New Testament,' concludes Dr Jaroslav Pelikan, 'Luther believed, was not a subjective thing, but the creation of the Creator Spirit Himself.'[67]

V

Luther firmly holds to the perspicuity of Scripture. He is convinced of its basic clarity. He assumes that each passage of

God's Word possesses one clear, definite and true sense of its own. *Scriptura sua radiat luce* was his slogan. 'There is not on earth a book more lucidly written than the Holy Scripture', he announces. 'Compared with all other books, it is as the sun compared with all other lights.'[68] It is his complaint against the Romanists that they persisted in regarding the Bible as a closed book, comprehended only by the ecclesiastical pundits. Whenever he sought to reprove them out of the Scripture, they raised the objection that its final interpretation is exclusively the prerogative of the Pope.[69] But Luther had to meet a similar obscurantist tendency in Erasmus. The great humanist of Rotterdam, whom Dr. Rupp wittily hails as the original Flying Dutchman because economic necessity compelled him to be 'in journeyings oft', seemed to overestimate the mysterious element in the Word. Whilst he acknowledged that 'the precepts destined to regulate our existence' were patent and evident, he found many other passages to be so obscure that no-one had ever unravelled them. Indeed, he went so far as to suggest that 'there are some sanctuaries in the Holy Scriptures into which God has not willed that we should enter too soon, and if we try to penetrate them we are surrounded with darkness.'[70] In his reply to Erasmus - *De Servo Arbitrio* as against *De Libero Arbitrio* - Luther is not slow to remark that by exaggerating the obscurity of Scripture his friend was guilty of resorting to the selfsame stratagem of traditional apologetic to which he had previously objected in the *Paraclesis* prefixed to his edition of the Greek Testament. There Erasmus had wholeheartedly dissented from those who refused to place the Scriptures in the hands of unlearned and ignorant men and had hoped rather that they might be read and understood not only by the Scots and Irish, but also by the Turks and Saracens, by the ploughboy, the weaver and the traveller. Luther vehemently denies that the Scriptures are abstruse. 'It is with such scarecrows that Satan has frightened away men from reading the Sacred Writings, and has rendered the Holy Scriptures contemptible, that he might cause his poison of philosophy to prevail in the Church.'[71] And so he claims 'that no part of Holy Scripture is dark... Christ hath not so enlightened us that any part of His doctrine and His Word which He bids us regard and follow should be left in the dark'.[72] In Luther's opinion, the Diatribe of Erasmus 'not being able to endure the brightness, nay the lightning of the most clear Scriptures, pretending by every kind of manoeuvre that it does not see (which is the truth of the case) wishes to persuade us that our eyes are also covered that we cannot see'.[73] Elsewhere in *De Servo Arbitrio* Luther refers emphatically to 'the all clear Scriptures of God' and 'the all clear light of the Scripture'.[73]

Luther argues that the perspicuity of Scripture is evidenced by the way in which throughout the Christian centuries devout scholars have based their arguments upon it and drawn their proof-texts from it. 'The Holy Scriptures must needs be clearer, easier of interpretation and more certain than any other scriptures, for all teachers prove their statements by them, as by clearer and more stable writings, and wish their own writings to be established and explained by them. But no-one can ever prove a dark saying by one that is still darker; therefore, necessity compels us to run to the Bible with all the writings of the doctors, and thence to get our verdict and judgment upon them; for Scripture alone is the true overlord and master of all writings on earth. If not, what are the Scriptures good for? Let us reject them and be satisfied with the books of men and human teachers.'[75] If we cannot look to the Bible for the light of knowledge, where else shall we find it? Luther accuses Erasmus of abandoning men to the broken light of human wisdom by buttressing as he does the orthodox doctrine of Scriptural obscurity. 'And you, too, my friend Erasmus, know very well what you are saying, when you deny that the Scripture is clear, for you at the same time drop in my ear this assertion: "it of necessity follows therefore, that all your saints, whom you adduce, are much less clear". And truly it would be so. For who shall certify us concerning their light, if you make the Scriptures obscure? Therefore they who deny the all-clearness and all-plainness of Scripture, leave us nothing else but darkness.'[76]

It is from this point of view that Luther registers his complaint about the many 'commentaries and books' through which 'the dear Bible is being buried and covered up so that no-one takes note of the text'. He refers to his own experience. 'When I was young, I familiarized myself with the Bible, read it often, and became well-acquainted with the text; so well that I knew where every passage that was mentioned was to be found: thus I became a *bonus textualis*. Not till then did I read the commentators. But finally I had to disregard them all and put them away because the use of them did not satisfy my conscience, and I had to take my stand again on the Bible; for it is much better to see with your own eyes than with another's.[77] In his Preface to Romans Luther speaks in the same strain: 'For heretofore it (i.e. the Epistle) has been evilly darkened with commentaries and all kinds of idle talk, though it is, in itself, a bright light, almost enough to illumine all the Scripture.'[78] No book, not even a book about the Book, can match the Book itself. 'You shall know', writes Luther, in the preface to the first volume of the 1539 edition of his German works, 'that the holy Scripture is such a book that it makes the wisdom of all other books foolishness, whilst it also teaches eternal life.'[79]

This insistence on the self-explanatory clarity of Scripture released the Book from bondage to the experts. A similar emancipation is overdue today. The Roman dogma of Scriptural obscurity and oligarchical interpretation reappears in another form. Instead of the Pope and his doctors we now meet those specialists in the history of the biblical period who would imply that without an acquaintance with the contemporary background it is impossible even for the simple believer to grasp the meaning of the Word. So, to borrow Luther's own vivid phrase, they 'hatch the eggs and become our idol'. This is not to suggest, of course, that the researches of our scholars are in vain. They possess an incalculable apologetic value and we are perpetually indebted to them. But it must not therefore be assumed that an adequate understanding of Scripture depends upon our familiarity with its secular historical context. The only background really necessary for a reliable and sufficient comprehension of Scripture is provided by Scripture itself.[80] Hence Luther's repeated warning against the danger of substituting human interpretation for the text, i.e. the clear words of Scripture itself. 'With the text and from the foundation of the Holy Scriptures I have silenced and slain all my opponents. For whoever is well founded and practised in the text will become a good and fine theologian, since a passage, or text, from the Bible has more weight than many commentators and glosses, which are not strong and round and do not help in the controversy.'[81] Hence his advice to his pupils is this: 'Do not permit yourselves to be led out of, and away from Scripture, no matter how hard they (the papists) may try. For if you step out of scripture, you are lost: then they will lead you just as they wish. But if you remain in Scripture, you have won the victory and you will regard their raging in no other way than when the crag of the sea smiles at the waves and billows. All their writings are nothing else than waves that rock to and fro. Be assured and certain that there is nothing clearer than the sun, I mean, Holy Scripture. If a cloud drifts before it, nothing else than the same clear sun is nevertheless behind it.'[82]

That last quotation makes it evident that whilst asserting the fundamental clarity of Scripture, Luther does not deny that there are passages hard to be understood. 'This indeed I confess, that there are many *places* in the Scriptures obscure and abstruse; not from the majesty of the things, but from our ignorance of certain terms and grammatical particulars; but which do not prevent a knowledge of all the *things* in the Scriptures.'[83] Luther distinguishes between the intelligibility of the contents of Scripture and the clarity of words through which this revealed content is communicated. Mysteries there must be, for finite reason cannot hope to climb up into the majesty of the divine. The things of God will not be fully comprehensible to the human mind, but the things of Scripture are always clear. In other words, although the 'how' may be concealed, the 'that' remains unambiguously plain. 'Scripture simply confesses the Trinity of God, the humanity of Christ, and the unpardonable sin. There is here no obscurity or ambiguity whatever. But how these things are, Scripture does not say, nor is it necessary to be known. The sophists employ their dreams here; attack and condemn them, and acquit Scripture.'[84] And so in a resoundingly triumphant passage Luther can provide the conclusion of the whole matter. 'For what thing of more importance can remain hidden in the Scriptures, now that the seals are broken, the stone rolled away from the door of the sepulchre, and that greatest of all mysteries brought to light, Christ made man: that God is Trinity and Unity: that Christ suffered for us and will reign to all eternity? Are not these things known and proclaimed even in our streets?'[85]

VI

A further hermeneutical principle follows logically from Luther's assertion of the perspicuity of Scripture. It is crystallized in the phrase, *Scriptura sui ipsius interpres.* 'That is the true method of interpretation,' says Luther, 'which puts Scripture alongside of Scripture in a right and proper way.'[87] He effectively employs the comparative technique by setting one portion of the Word beside another and allowing the plainer texts to illuminate the more difficult, as Origen, Jerome and Augustine had recommended.[88] Luther acknowledges his indebtedness to the past when he writes: 'The holy Fathers explained Scripture by taking the clear, lucid passages and with them shed light on obscure and doubtful passages.'[89] 'In this manner', he tells us, 'Scripture is its own light. It is a fine thing when Scripture explains itself.'[90]

In laying down the rule that 'one passage must be explained by another', Luther adds immediately, 'namely, a doubtful and obscure passage must be explained by a clear and certain passage'.[91] Obviously, the clear passage needs no explanation, although, of course, it may be corroborated by other Scriptures. In his controversy with the *Schwärmer* or 'Enthusiasts' Luther had occasion to object to their habit of obscuring what was already sufficiently plain by further comparisons. Behind their spurious exegesis of John vi, for instance, there lies the misconception that even the clear must be further elaborated. Luther repudiates such a work of exegetical supererogation. 'The result of this method will be that no passage in Scripture will remain certain and clear, and the comparison of one passage with another will never end... To demand that clear and certain passages be explained by drawing in other passages amounts to an iniquitous deriding of the truth and injection of fog into the light. If one set out to explain all passages by first comparing them with other passages, he would be reducing the whole of Scripture to a vast and uncertain chaos.'[92]

This formula of Scripture as its own interpreter is closely linked with another - that all exposition should be in accordance with the analogy of faith. The use of this term by Luther and the reformers generally is in fact a misapplication of its original occurrence in Romans xii. 6. 'The expression *propheteian kata ten analogian tes pisteos'*, comments Denney in the *Expositor's Greek Testament*, 'implies that the more faith one has - the more completely Christian he is - the greater the prophetic endowment will be.' He adds that 'in theology "the analogy of faith" is used in quite a different sense, though it was supposed to be justified by this passage. To interpret Scripture e.g. according to the analogy of faith, meant to interpret the parts, especially difficult or obscure parts, in consistency with the whole. The scope of the whole, again, was supposed to be represented in the Creed or Rule of Faith; and to interpret *kata ten analogian tes pisteos* meant simply not to run counter to the Creed.' Denney concludes somewhat curtly: 'In the passage before us this is an anachronism as well as an irrelevance.'[93]

However inappropriate the term *analogia fidei* may be to reflect the apostle's intention, it is nevertheless useful to delineate Luther's own attitude. For him the rule of faith is the Scripture itself. No extraneous canon is invoked. He finds his sufficient criterion within the Word of God. Creeds and confessions are only of value in so far as they embody the rule of

Scripture. But he demands that reference must be made to the Scripture as a whole and not merely to selected parts of it. 'It behoves a theologian, if he would avoid error, to have regard to the whole of Scripture and compare contraries with contraries.'[94] The sophists, indeed, 'support themselves with Scripture, because they would look laughable if they tried to force their own dreams on men; but they do not quote Scripture in its entirety. They always snatch up what appears to favour them; but what is against them they either cleverly conceal or corrupt with their cunning glosses'.[95] That is why Luther can call the Bible a heresy book, because the mere citation of texts without recourse to the rule of faith may be so engineered as to give the impression of vindicating the most extreme heterodoxy. What Luther means by *analogia fidei* is neatly expressed by James Wood when he says that 'the interpretation has to be congruent with the general norm of the Word of God'.[96]

This is something radically different, however, from Schleiermacher's *das Schriftganze* by which he claimed that the Christian articles of faith must not be drawn from those Scriptures which treat of separate doctrines, but only from the general scope and tenor of the Bible. He contended that 'it is a most precarious procedure to quote Scripture passages in dogmatic treatises and, besides, in itself, quite inadequate'.[97] Luther was equally conscious of the peril involved. He disapproved of the indiscriminate concatenation of Bible verses without due respect to their meaning and context. 'Heretofore I have held that where something was to be proved by the Scriptures, the Scriptures quoted must really refer to the point at issue. I learn now that it is not enough to throw many passages together helter-skelter whether they fit or not. If this is to be the way, then I can easily prove from the Scriptures that beer is better than wine.'[98] But, as Mueller brings out, Schleiermacher's application of *das Schriftganze* was only a pretext to excuse his thoroughly unscriptural method of deriving theological truths from reason or the pious self-consciousness. Kliefoth was surely justified in dismissing this alleged disparity between the part and the whole in Scripture, as represented in Schleiermacher and Hofmann after him, as an 'inconceivable concept'.[99]

Luther displays a recognition of the unity of Scripture which is startlingly up-to-date. It severs him from many interpreters in the eighteenth and nineteenth centuries and links him with some of the most recent trends. He found no difficulty in interpreting the New Testament in the light of the Old, and the

Old Testament in the light of the New. For him the two sections of Scripture constitute a single entity. He would subscribe to the dictum of Augustine that the New Testament is latent in the Old and the Old Testament patent in the New.[100] Not only does the New Testament form a unit with the Old Testament: it is also a unit within itself. Despite the individual preferences which he expressed and of which much (too much) has been made by the undiscerning, there is no real ground for surmising that Luther recognized any serious inequality between the various volumes received into the Canon. 'To conceive of the New Testament in such a way and to split it up into different sections of unequal worth', observes Professor Aland, 'would be fundamentally to misunderstand Luther.'[101] There follows a quotation from Luther's Preface to the New Testament to indicate his unequivocal opinion. 'Therefore let it first be known that we must rid ourselves of the delusion that there are four Gospels and only four Gospels.... on the contrary, we must adhere to this.... the New Testament is one book, in which are written the Gospel and God's promise, as well as the history of those who believed and those who did not. Thus every man may be sure that there is only one Gospel, only one book in the New Testament, only one faith, and only one God Who promises (salvation).'[102]

VII

One of the most valuable of Luther's hermeneutical principles is his insistence on the primacy of the literal sense. He resolutely sets aside the verbal jugglery involved in multiple exegesis and firmly takes his stand upon the plain and obvious significance of the Word. 'The literal sense of Scripture alone', he asserts, 'is the whole essence of faith and Christian theology.'[103] And again: 'If we wish to handle Scripture aright, our sole effort will be to obtain the one, simple, seminal and certain literal sense.'[104]

This meant the rejection of what Dean Farrar dubbed 'the fatal dream' of the fourfold sense, so dear to the Medieval Schoolmen.[105] Scripture was expounded by means of the *Quadriga,* or fourfold rule, around which, according to Guibert of Nogent, every sacred page revolved as on wheels.[106] Luther himself explains it: 'In the schools of theologians it is a well-known rule that Scripture is to be understood in four ways, literal, allegorical, moral, anagogical.'[107] 'The literal meaning speaks of acts, the allegorical of what you believe, the moral of what you do, the anagogical of what you hope.'[108] The text was held to contain a double meaning, literal and spiritual. The spiritual sense was further subdivided into the moral or tropological sense applied to the individual believer, the allegorical to the Church and the anagogical to the future. Since so much capital has been made out of the abuses to which this type of exegesis was prone, it ought to be observed that throughout the Middle Ages and into the period of the Reformation only the literal sense was valid in disputations and in exegesis it was not considered essential to search for all four possibilities in every verse. Whatever its weaknesses, this discipline at least provided an incentive to examine the text thoroughly from a variety of angles.

As we shall see later, Luther did not altogether set aside spiritual interpretation, but he emphatically urged the priority and superiority of the literal sense. For a thousand years the Church had buttressed its theological edifice by means of an authoritative exegesis which depended upon allegory as its chief medium of interpretation. Luther struck a mortal blow at this vulnerable spot. From his own experience he knew the futility of allegorization: 'mere jugglery', 'a merry game', 'monkey tricks' - that is how he stigmatizes it.[109] He had suffered much from that sort of psuedo-exposition of which Dr. John Lowe speaks so trenchantly, where 'anything can mean anything'.[110] 'When I was a monk,' Luther frankly acknowleges, 'I was an adept in allegory. I allegorized everything. But after lecturing on the Epistle to the Romans, I came to have some knowledge of Christ. For therein I saw that Christ is no allegory, and learned to know what Christ was.'[111] His emancipation was only gradual, for there are occasions, especially in his lectures on the Psalms, when we catch him relapsing into his former style. 'It was very difficult for me to break away from my habitual zeal for allegory', he confides. 'And yet I was aware that allegories were empty speculations and the froth, as it were, of the Holy Scriptures. It is the historical sense alone which supplies the true and sound doctrine.'[112] In thus attempting to reinstate the *sensus literalis* Luther was, in fact, continuing a tradition which had never been altogether buried. Thomas Aquinas had upheld it and before him Albertus Magnus and Richard of St. Victor. Nicholas of Lyra more immediately prepared the path for Luther: hence the jingle:

> *Si Lyra non lyrasset*
> *Lutherus non saltasset.*

But it was a long time before Luther recognized the worth of Lyra's contribution.

Luther does not altogether abandon allegory, for in the passage quoted above (which is from his late lectures on Genesis) he adds: 'After this (i.e. the literal sense) has been treated and correctly understood, then one may also employ allegories as an adornment and flowers to embellish and illuminate the account. The bare allegories, which stand in no relation to the account, and do not illuminate it, should simply be disapproved (rejected) as empty dreams... Therefore let those who want to make use of allegories base them on the historical account itself.'[113]

Luther's stress on the literal sense is related to his belief in the perspicuity of Scripture. He holds that the Word of God has 'one simple, direct, indisputable meaning, on which our faith may rest without wavering'.[114] 'The Holy Spirit is the plainest writer and speaker in heaven and earth,' he says, ' and therefore His words cannot have more than one, and that the very simplest sense, which we call the literal, ordinary, natural sense.'[115] So in his own exegesis he sets out to discover 'the simple sense of His simple words'.[116] In the lectures on Genesis he winds up his exposition of the first three chapters by claiming that according to his ability he has treated the contents in their historical meaning, which he believes to be their real and true one. He dissociates himself from what he calls 'the ridiculous procedure' which Origen and Jerome pursued in expounding these same chapters, for they departed from the historical account to enquire after a spiritual meaning of which they had no knowledge. Augustine, too, was not irreproachable in this respect. To subject the text to such fanciful elaboration is, Luther feels, a desecration of the sacred writers. He therefore concludes that 'in the interpretation of Holy Scripture the main task must be to derive from it some sure and plain meaning'.[117]

His chief objection to the heavenly prophets of Zwickau was that they spiritualized away the literal sense of Scripture. 'Brother,' - so he addresses Carlstadt - 'the natural meaning of the words is queen, transcending all subtle, acute, sophistical fancy. From it we may not deviate unless compelled by a clear article of the faith. Otherwise the spiritual jugglers would not have a single letter in Scripture. Therefore, interpretations of God's Word must be lucid and definite, having a firm, sure, and true foundation on which one may confidently rely.'[118] Erasmus is rebuked for the same tendency. 'When shall we ever have any plain and pure text, without tropes and conclusions, either for or against freewill? Has the Scripture no such texts anywhere? And shall the cause of free will remain for ever in doubt, like a reed shaken with the wind, as being that which can be supported by no certain text, but which stands upon conclusions and tropes only, introduced by men mutually disagreeing with each other? But let our sentiment be this:- that neither conclusion nor trope is to be admitted into the Scriptures, unless the evident state of the particulars, or the absurdity of any particular as militating against an article of faith, require it: but, that the simple, pure and natural meaning of the words is to be adhered to, which is according to the rules of grammar and to that common use of speech which God has given to men.'[119] And this too, of course, is the offence of the Romanists who, according to Luther, toss the words of God to and fro, as gamblers throw their dice, and 'take from the Scriptures their single, simple, constant sense'.[120]

Luther apparently prefers to speak of the grammatical and historical rather than the literal sense, although it is evident that the three terms are intimately related.[121] In his own exegesis he usually puts into practice the precepts he has enjoined upon others, especially in respect of the principle at present under review. It will be worthwhile to watch him at work. His first procedure is to determine the semantic range of the particular passage before him. He examines it in relation to its context. He endeavours to expound it in congruity with the over-all design of the chapter and book in which it occurs. For example, in dealing with the fifth Psalm, he immediately sets aside what Lyra and the other commentators have written and considers what is the intention of the Holy Spirit through the Psalmist as indicated in the text itself. 'It is certain that this Psalm does not treat of sufferings and tribulations, for David (lit. the person who harps) does not say one word about them. The whole Psalm is a complaint concerning the ungodly, the unjust, and the wicked. The scope of the Psalm, therefore, according to my judgment, is this:- the prophet is praying against hypocrites, deceitful workers, and false prophets, who seduce and deceive the people of God and the heritage of Christ by their human traditions; whom Christ calls in Matthew vii "ravening wolves" and the apostle in Titus i : 10 "vain talkers and deceivers".' And Luther explains that, as in the preceding Psalm David inveighed against a mere profession of righteousness in the realm of practice, so here he attacks the same abuse in the realm of doctrine. 'We shall therefore find that this Psalm is directed against all false prophets, hypocrites, heretics, superstitious ones and the whole generation of those who devour the people of God by an adulteration of His Word, and by a false show of works.'[122]   It is interesting that Luther's interpretation is confirmed by more recent commentators. Professor Kirkpatrick, for instance, describes this fifth Psalm as 'a morning prayer uttered by one who is exposed to danger from the machinations of unscrupulous and hypocritical enemies'.[123]

In his initial approach to the text Luther also considers its relationship to the rule of faith. He attempts to envisage it in the light of the total content of Scripture and to define its precise position in the harmony of truth. In order to understand any portion of the Word it is necessary to know what is taught by the Word as a whole. 'Scripture is indeed the rule of doctrine,' - so Paulsen expounds Luther's principle here - 'but, *vice versa*, doctrine is also the rule of Scripture which must be interpreted *ex analogia fidei*.'[124] Nevertheless, having ascertained the general scope of the passage before him, Luther then concerns himself with the elucidation of the philological and syntactic sense. He says he tries to observe the rule never to fight against the grammar. He makes it quite clear, however, that this is a subsidiary investigation, the value of which depends entirely upon the contribution it makes towards establishing the true meaning of the text. 'Therefore in every exposition the subject should be given consideration first; that is, it must be determined what is under consideration. After this has been done, the next step is that the words should be adapted to the matter if the character of the language so permits, not the matter to the words.'[125] In dealing with the *crux exegetica* in Genesis iv. 13 he complains that previous commentators have been misled by a restricted philological method divorced from the necessary cooperation of theology. Hence the learned Dominican, Pagnino, had offered the translation (as does our Authorized Version), 'My punishment is greater than I can bear.' But, as Luther pithily puts it, this is to make a martyr out of Cain and a sinner out of Abel, so he strikingly renders Cain's *cri de coeur* as, 'My iniquity is greater than can be forgiven.' 'Thus we see that philologists who are nothing but philologists,' he concludes, 'and have no knowledge of theological matters have their perplexing difficulties with such passages and torture not only Scripture but also themselves and their hearers. First the meaning should be established in such a manner that it is everywhere in agreement, and then philology should be brought into play.'[126]

It is noteworthy that in treating Genesis iv. 13 Luther strives to vindicate his interpretation, whether successfully or otherwise, by a careful and comparative study of the vocabulary involved. That is quite characteristic of his method. He is at pains to uncover the precise significance of each word. And it must be remembered that Luther's linguistic equipment was by no means negligible. He had studied Hebrew through Reuchlin's *Rudimenta* from 1509 and Greek from 1511. He had devoted himself to a monumental project of translation. In his *Essay on Translating* he recounts how he and two of his helpers once spent four days over three lines in the Book of Job.[127] We are not altogether surprised, then, that he should lay it down that 'to expound Scripture, to interpret it rightly and to fight against those people who quote wrongly... cannot be done without knowledge of the languages'.[128] But it is Luther's consistent objective through the right interpretation of the dead languages to arrive at the living message.

VIII

Luther fearlessly advanced the literal sense in the face of his opponents. Nowhere is this more apparent than in his controversy with Jerome Emser, Secretary to Duke George of Saxony and a Court Chaplain. (Luther addresses him unceremoniously as the Leipzig Goat - a dual allusion both to his escutcheon and his belligerency - and tells him that he must not defile the Holy Scriptures with his snout.) As Steimle has noted, 'Luther goes straight to the fundamental difference between them, the sole authority of Scripture in matters of faith and the right exposition of Scripture according to its grammatical sense. Over against Emser's position, that he would fight with the sword - i.e. the Word of truth - but that he would not permit it to remain in the scabbard of the word sense, but use the naked blade of the spiritual sense, Luther, in the most important section of his answer, under the subtitle "The Letter and the Spirit", utters the foundation principles of Protestant exegesis.'[129]

This crucial insertion must now occupy our attention. It represents a most important segment in the core documentation of Luther's hermeneutics. Augustine had penned a treatise against Pelagius carrying the same title. It was from Augustine, perhaps through Lefevre, that Luther derived his own distinction between spirit and letter. As Quanbeck says, it became one of the basic elements in his principles of interpretation, although he tempered it somewhat by the strong historical tendency of his thought.[130] Emser took as his text 2 Corinthians iii. 6 ('the letter killeth, but the spirit giveth life') and argued that anyone who understands Scripture only according to the letter and not according to the spirit had better turn to Virgil or some other heathen tale, for he will read only to his own destruction. He accused Luther of this very failure and consequently regarded him as merely beating the air with the scabbard instead of fighting with the sword itself.[131] Luther follows Augustine in explaining that the apostle's words do not refer primarily to modes of speech but to the explicit prohibition of evil by the Law. "'The letter killeth, the spirit giveth life" might be expressed in other words, thus: "The Law killeth, but the grace of God giveth life": or, "Grace gives help and does all that the Law demands and of itself cannot do."'[132] Indeed Luther actually quotes from Augustine - a fine sentence, as he calls it, from the commentary on Psalm xvii where he provides 'this happy and striking explanation, "the letter is none other than law apart from grace."' 'And so we may also say', Luther adds, 'the spirit is none other than grace apart from the Law.'[133] We must not overlook the fact, however, that Augustine does not altogether rule out the application of 2 Corinthians iii. 6 to the subject of interpretation: the sense may also fit that, he says in parenthesis.[134] Luther challenges Emser's contention as being unscriptural. He will recognize no hermeneutical method which is not itself derived from the Word. He boldly invites Emser to produce a single letter in the whole Bible that agrees with his magnification of the spiritual sense.[135] He proposes to put Emser to school with Paul in order that he may learn what is really intended by this distinction between the spirit and the letter. As it is, Emser has no conception of Paul's meaning. 'How well Emser agrees with St. Paul: like a donkey singing a duet with a nightingale.'[136] We must not create mysteries where the Scripture does not indicate them: only the Spirit 'speaketh mysteries' (1 Cor. xiv. 2). Hence he argues that Emser's spiritual sense is inadmissible in controversy, as all the Schoolmen agreed, 'but the other sense is the highest, best, strongest; in short, it is the whole substance, essence and foundation of Scripture, so that if the literal sense were taken away, all the Scriptures would be nothing.'[137] Instead of venturing too far and too high, like foolish chamois hunters, 'it is much surer and safer to abide by the words in their simple sense; they furnish the real pasture and right dwelling-places for all minds.'[138] Luther comes to the uncomplimentary conclusion that the text in 2 Corinthians iii squares with Emser's twofold sense, spiritual and literal, as perfectly as his head does with the profundities of philosophy.[129] He will have nothing to do with this double Bible which casts uncertainty upon the truth of God.[140]

Luther then proceeds to expound at some length the true significance of the letter and the spirit in relation to the two ministries of the law and the gospel. But it is to be observed that here and elsewhere in his writings Luther does not relate these inflexibly to the division between the Testaments, as was the current fashion. It is not a matter of equating law with the Old Testament and gospel with the New. On the contrary, he asserts that without the light of the Spirit the whole of Scripture is law, and with the light of the Spirit the whole of Scripture is gospel. 'Where the Spirit is present', he says, 'all Scripture is saving.'[141] The distinction between letter and spirit, then, is, as Prenter has reminded us, 'absolutely attached to the motion of faith away from man himself toward Christ. Those who understand the Gospel in a proud and false way are selfishly changing it into a *verbum imperfectum et longum*, to an empty and useless and false word, no matter how the word itself is the high and holy Gospel. The Word, however, which truly is *verbum spiritus,* eliminates all pride and all egotism in the hearer. But such a word is only understood by faith. In this manner faith itself becomes a parabolically expounded, living *verbum abbreviatum.* The distinction between Law and Gospel is understood by this parabolic interpretation, not as a rigid dialectic point, but as the dynamic contrast which includes both the beginning and the end of the motion of faith'.[142] 'This is the difference between Law and Gospel,' says Luther himself, 'the Law is the word of Moses to us, the Gospel is the Word of God in us. The Law remains external, the Gospel is within.'[143] Thus when the law is received inwardly by faith it becomes gospel, and when the gospel is not received inwardly by faith it becomes law. The Word, then, as letter is law : as spirit it is gospel.

If we suspect that Luther has been reasoning in a circle here we shall be right. He has ushered the spirit sense out of the back door only to welcome it at the front. But it must be noted on what totally different terms it is now received. Emser's spiritual sense was derived from the tradition of the Church and rational processes. Luther's spiritual sense is derived from the Scripture itself and the apprehension of faith. So he can speak of the Spirit giving 'a new interpretation, which is then the new literal sense.'[144] Now that is a highly significant admission. It indicates that whilst, as we have seen, Luther maintains the primacy of the literal sense, he does not exclude a further interpretation. In his recognition of a *sensus plenior* he was perhaps nearer to Origen than he knew. Yet he would wish to gather everything within one meaning. After he has stated, in a passage already quoted, that since the Holy Spirit is the plainest of all speakers His words can only have one simple sense, the literal, he immediately adds: 'That the things indicated by the simple sense of His simple words should signify something further and different, and therefore one thing should always signify another, is more than a question of words or language. For the same is true of all other things outside of the Scriptures, since all of God's works and creatures are living signs and words of God, as St. Augustine and all the teachers declare.' 'But', he concludes, ' we are not to say that the Scriptures or the Word of God have more than one meaning.'[145] By way of illustration, Luther employs the analogy of a picture. A portrait of an actual man signifies that person without requiring any explanation. But that does not lead us to assume that the word 'picture' has a twofold sense, a literal sense (the picture) and a spiritual sense (the person). In the same way, Luther infers, the things in Scripture have a further significance, but the Scriptures do not on that account possess a double sense, but only the single yet comprehensive meaning the words themselves convey. It will be detected that Luther has borrowed from Augustine not only the distinction between *littera* and *spiritus* but also that between *signum* and *res*.[146]

Although, therefore, Luther urges the priority of the literal sense, it can hardly be said that to *sola Scriptura* he allies the further principle *sola historica sententia*, as Gerrish claims. Indeed, the latter goes on to admit that Luther allowed even the use of allegory, not as proof but as ornament and in accordance with the analogy of faith. In effect, Luther does concede a dual meaning of Scripture: or, at least two aspects of the same meaning. The Lutheran dogmaticians elaborated this unsystematized and at times inconsistent insight into a differentiation between the external and internal *forma* of Scripture. Quenstedt defines it thus: 'We must distinguish between the grammatical and outer meaning of the Divine Word and the spiritual, inner and Divine meaning of the Divine Word. The first is the *forma* of the Word of God insofar as it is a word, the latter is its *forma* insofar as it is a Divine Word.'[147] But we shall not altogether resolve this tension until we have examined another of Luther's hermeneutical principles.

Luther's interpretation of Scripture is at once Christocentric and Christological. It is Christocentric in that he regards the Lord Jesus Christ as the heart of the Bible. 'Take Christ out of the Scriptures and what will you find remaining in them?' he asks Erasmus.[148] 'In the whole Scripture there is nothing but Christ, either in plain words or involved words.'[149] 'The whole Scripture is about Christ alone everywhere, if we look to its inner meaning, though superficially it may sound different.'[150] Christ is 'the sun and truth in Scripture'.[151] He is the geometrical centre of the Bible.[152] He is the point from which the whole circle is drawn.[153] Scripture contains 'nothing but Christ and the Christian faith'.[154] And that categorical assertion obtains for the Old Testament as well as for the New, 'for it is beyond question that all the Scriptures point to Christ alone.'[155] 'The entire Old Testament refers to Christ and agrees with Him,' says Luther.[156]

In his Introduction to the Old Testament he pens this classic passage: 'Here you will find the swaddling clothes and the manger in which Christ lies. Simple and small are the swaddling clothes, but dear is the treasure, Christ, that lies in them.'[157] This Christocentric orientation of Scripture is raised to a major hermeneutical principle. 'If, then, you would interpret well and truly, set Christ before you,' Luther advises, 'for He is the man to Whom it all applies.'[158] And again, in his lectures on Romans: 'There a great stride has been made towards the right interpretation of Scripture, by understanding it all as bearing on Christ.'[159] It is in this context that we realize the discernment of Kramm's comment that for Luther the canon 'what urges Christ', in the much-quoted paragraph from his Preface to James and Jude, is a principle of interpretation, not of selection.[160]

Luther's Christocentric approach to Scripture supplies the clue to the paradox involved in his insistence on the primacy of the literal sense whilst conceding that there is a further, inner, spiritual meaning. Luther takes his stand on the literal sense. That is fundamental. But he recognises that there is an inward meaning of the Word to which the eyes of faith must penetrate. It is not supplementary to the literal sense but communicated by it. Luther's major contribution to hermeneutics lies in the fusion of literal and spiritual in a new and dynamic relationship. His view treats the Bible dialectically. It resolves the tension between the literal and the spiritual sense. It takes into account the interaction between the historical elements of Scripture. It transcends the normal categories of internal and external significance and achieves a vital synthesis between the letter and the spirit. This *rapprochement* is made possible because, as Blackman hints, for Luther Christ is both the literal and the spiritual sense of Scripture and these two are one in Him.[161] It is He who reconciles the apparently incompatible. The acknowledgement of Christ as Lord of Scripture provides the context in which the holy alliance of letter and spirit may be achieved.[162] In the first flush of his own discovery of this hermeneutical key, Luther could declare: 'Christ is the head of all the saints, the origin of all, the source of all streams... Therefore the words of Scripture concerning Christ at the same time share life with Him. And in this way all the four senses of Scripture flow into one.'[163] Later he would discard the *Quadriga* because of its misuse by Roman propagandists. But his Christocentric exegesis nevertheless ensured that full justice should be done to every intrinsic shade of meaning in Scripture.

That introduces us lastly to Luther's Christological conception of Scripture, which is determinative for his whole hermeneutical programme. His Christocentric perspective led him to affirm that, since Christ is the only revealer of God, He is the essential content of Scripture. But if the question be raised as to the mode of our Lord's manifestation in the Scriptures, Luther offers a profoundly constructive solution. As the divinity and power of God are embedded in the vessel of Christ's incarnate body, so the same divinity and power of God are embedded in Scripture, a vessel made of letters, composed of paper and printer's ink.[164] In order to grasp the biblical revelation in its fullness it is necessary to conceive of Scripture in terms of the divine-human nature of Christ.[165]

Luther's recognition of this incarnational factor in the doctrine of Scripture is one of his most relevant insights and conditions the necessary presupposition of his hermeneutics about which we spoke earlier. The clue to Luther's biblical interpretation is the Christological method of Scripture itself. The very categories he employs are Christological rather than scientific, philosophical or even narrowly theological. For him the basic hermeneutical problem is the reconciliation of the divine and human elements of Scripture. The Bible is God's Book. Its writers were God-inspired men. Through it God still speaks. But the writers were also human and what they wrote has been recorded in the normal fashion. Luther realized that the problem raised is Christological at the core. His argument stems from the statement, *Scriptura sacra est Deus incarnatus.* He draws a deliberate analogy between scripture and the Person of Christ, between the Word written and the Word made flesh. 'And the Word', he says, 'is just like the Son of God.'[166] As in the doctrine of the incarnation the Church announces that our Lord was at once fully God and fully man, so Luther would have us maintain the full divinity and full humanity, as it were of Holy Scripture. The Chalcedonian formula concerning the two natures of Christ is also to be applied to the Bible. Moreover, Luther relates his concept of *communicatio idiomatum* (see p. 107) to the Scriptures, as well as to the Person of Christ and the sacraments, thus safeguarding the unity of the Bible from arbitrary fragmentation.[167] What is predicated of one element pertains to the other: there is a sort of interpenetration. All this throws valuable light on the nature of Scripture and constitutes a contribution of major importance to the field represented by Scharlemann's first hermeneutical circle.

But its precise definition by Luther must be carefully observed. In recognizing that Scripture is both human and divine he does not thereby open the door to the suggestion of fallibility. He presses the analogy between the incarnation and Scripture to its utmost logical limit in what we have called his Christological approach. The human element of the Bible is no more liable to error than was the human nature of Christ. He scrupulously avoids the charge of what we might describe as Biblical Nestorianism. 'Luther was well aware of the human side of Scripture,' writes Dr. Pieper, 'but only in the sense that God caused His Word to be written by men in a human tongue. He is horrified at people who dare assert that Scripture is not entirely and in all its parts the Word of God, because the writers, such as Peter and Paul, after all were men.'[168] Commenting on 1 Peter iii. 15, Luther remarks: 'But if they take exception and say, You preach that one should not hold man's doctrine and yet Peter and Paul and even Christ were men - when you hear people of this stamp who are so blinded and hardened as to deny that which Christ and the apostles spoke and wrote in God's Word, or doubt it, then be silent, speak no more with them and let them go.'[169] It is within the sanctions imposed by such a conception that the whole of Luther's hermeneutics move.

This cursory and all too inadequate survey of an extensive corpus of hermeneutical material may at least serve to underline the pivotal significance of Luther's biblical interpretation and its relevance to current discussions. We close as we began with a quotation from Professor Grant's *The Bible in the Church*. Our investigations will have in some measure substantiated his claim that Luther's contribution in this sphere has 'permanent value for the interpretation of Scripture. Today the reviving theological interpretation of the Bible must look to him'.[170]

REFERENCES

1. R.M. Grant, *The Bible in the Church*, p.109.
2. M. Luther, *Werke*, Weimer Auflage (W.A.), II, p.279.
3. H.E. Jacobs, *Luther* in E.R.E. VIII, p.201.
4. W.A., VII, p.838.
5. R.H. Bainton. *Here I Stand*, p.185.
6. J. Kuehn, *Luther und der Wormser Reichstag*, p.75, n.4.
7. H. Jedin, *History of the Council of Trent*. I, p.171.
8. E.G. Schwiebert, *Luther and His Times*, p.351.
9. R.H. Murray, *Erasmus and Luther*, p.145.
10. M. Luther, *Works*, ed. J. Pelikan (P.E.), XXXI, 266, 267.
11. Bainton, *op. cit.*, pp. 95,96.
12. A. Harnack, *Dogmengeschichte*, III, p.665.
13. W.A., VI, pp.316,321.
14. *ibid.*, p.305.
15. M. Luther, *Works*, Holman Edition (H.E.), III p.90.
16. H.E., I, p.29. 17. *ibid.*
18. *ibid.*, p.16.
19. W.A. Quanbeck, *Luther Today: Martin Luther Lectures I*, p.37.
20. T.Stork, *Luther and the Bible*, p.iii.
21. Schwiebert, *op. cit.*, p.288.
22. More likely than Erfurt - cf. Schwiebert, *op. cit.*, pp.121, 122.
23. W.A., LIV, pp. 185, 187.
24. W. Schwarz, *The Problem of Biblical Translation*, p.169.
25. *ibid.*
26. M. Luther, *Works*, ed. J.N. Lenker (L.E.), II, p.429.
27. W.A., x, p.1062. 28. L.E., II, p.455.
29. R. Prenter, *Spiritus Creator*, p.XVI.
30. H.S. Nash, 'Hermeneutics' in *New Schaff-Herzog Encyclopaedia*, IV, p.244.
31. *The Letters of Martin Luther*, ed. M. Currie, p.196.
32. G. Ebeling, *Evangelische Evangeliensauslegung*, p.13.
33. J.W. Heikinnen, 'Luther's Lectures on the Romans,' *Interpretation*, VII, 180.
34. R. Seeberg, *Lehrbuch der Dogmengeschichte*, II, 289.
35. MS paper kindly loaned.
36. G.H. Schodde, 'Interpretation' in *International Standard Bible Encyclopaedia*, III *in loc.*
37. M. Luther, *Works*, St. Louis Edition (St. L.) IX, p.1818.
38. *ibid.*, p.1800.
39. St. L., III, p.1890; VI, p.2095; III, p.1895.
40. cf. F. Pieper, *Christian Dogmatics*, I, p.278.
41. B.S. Gerrish, 'Biblical Authority and the Continental Reformation' in *S.J.T.*, x, 346.
42. J.D. Wood, *The Interpretation of the Bible*, p.88.
43. P.E., XIII, p.17. 44. L.E. I, p.57.
45. W.A., VII p.97.
46. *Dr. Martin Luther's Briefwechsel*, eds. E.L. Enders and G. Kawerau, I, p.141.
47. W.A., VII, p.546.

48. W.A., LVII, p.185; cf. XV, p.565.
49. P.E., XXII, p.8.   50. W.A., IV, p.519.
51. *Letters*, p.178.   52. P.E., XXII, p.6.
53. M. Luther, *Werke*, Erlangen Edition (E.E.), XV, p.144.
54. W.A., XLII, p.35.
55. cf. J.T. Mueller, *Christian Dogmatics*, p.127.
56. H.H. Kramm, *The Theology of Martin Luther*, p.109.
57. L.E., XII, pp. 16, 17.   58. *Luther Today*, p.101.
59. H.E., III, p.127.
60. J. Calvin, *Institutes*, I.vii. 5.
61. W.A., III p.549.   62. W.A., v, p.108.
63. E.E., LVII, p.16.   64. Grant *op. cit.*, p.113.
65. W.A., XVIII, p. 1588.   66. Grant, *op. cit.*, pp.116, 117.
67. P.E., XXI, xiv.   68. M. Luther, *Comment on Psalm 37*.
69. W.A., VI, p.406.
70. Quoted in E.G. Rupp, *The Righteousness of God*, p.272.
71. M. Luther, *The Bondage of the Will*, ed. H. Cole, p.25.
72. M. Luther, *Werke*, Walch Edition, XVIII, pp. 2163-2164.
73. *Bondage*, p.236   74. *ibid.*, pp.27, 290.
75. H.E., III, p.16.   76. *Bondage*, p.109.
77. St. L., XXII, pp.54,55.   78. H.E., VI, p.447.
79. W.A., I, p.659.   80. cf. Pieper, *op. cit.*, I, pp. 365,366.
81. E.E., LVI, p.7.   82. St. L., V, p.334.
83. *Bondage*, pp.25,26.   84. St. L., XVIII, pp. 1682ff.
85. *Bondage*, p.26.   86. W.A., VII, p.97.
87. H.E., III, p.334.
88. cf. Origen, *De Principiis*, IV; Augustine, *De Doctrina* I-III; Jerome, *Ad Paulum Ep.* 1iii, 6.7.
89. St. L., XX, p.856.   90. St. L., XI, p.2335.
91. St. L., V, p.335.   92. St. L., XX, p.325.
93. *E.G.T.* II, *in loc.*
94. M. Luther, *Opera Latina*, ed. H. Schmidt, III, p.185.
95. P.E., I, p.107.   96. Wood, *op. cit.*, p.89
97. F.D.E. Schleiermacher, *Glaubenslehre*, I, p.30.
98. W.A., VI, p.301.   99. Quoted in Pieper, *op. cit.*, I, p.201.
100. Augustine, *Quaestionum in Heptateuchum*, II, 73.
101. K. Aland, 'Luther as Exegete' in *Expository Times*, LXIX, p.70.
102. W.A., VI, p.2.
103. Quoted in F.W. Farrar, *History of Interpretation*, p.327.
104. *ibid.*   105. *ibid.* p. 267.
106. Guibert of Nogent, 'How to Make a Sermon' in *Early Medieval Theology*, ed. G.E. McCracken and A. Cabaniss (L.C.C. IX), p.291.
107. Farrar, *op. cit.*, p.327.   108. *Luther Today*, p.62.
109. H.E., III, p. 334: Farrar, *op cit.*, p.328.
110. *The Interpretation of the Bible*, ed. C.W. Dugmore, p.121.
111. W.A., I, p.136.   112. W.A., XLII, p.173.
113. *ibid.*   114. H.E., I, p.370.
115. H.E., III, p.350.   116. *ibid.*
117. P.E., I, p.231; cf. p.232.   118. P.E., XL, p.190.
119. *Bondage*, p.205.   120. H.E., III, p.37.
121. H.E., II, 189; III, p.352.
122. M. Luther, *Commentary on the First Twenty-two Psalms*, ed. H. Cole, I, pp.177,178.

123. A.F. Kirkpatrick, *Psalms*, I, p.20.
124. F. Paulsen, *Geschichte*, I, p.199.
125. P.E., I, p.263.
126. *ibid.* p.298. Luther's rendering of Genesis iv. 13 is supported by RV mg.
127. H.E., V, p. 14.
128. *Luther Speaks*, ed. H.P. Ehrenberg, p.72.
129. H.E., III, pp. 279, 280.   130. *Luther Today*, p.47.
131. H.E., III, p.319.   132. *ibid.* p.356.
133. *ibid.* p.362.
134. Augustine, *De Spiritu et Littera*, V, 7. Luther declares: 'In that passage St. Paul does not write one iota about these two senses' (H.E., III, p.353).
135. H.E., III, p.352.   136. *ibid.*, p.348.
137. *ibid.*, p.349.   138. *ibid.*, p.350.
139. *ibid.*, p.353.   140. *ibid.*, p.351.
141. Quoted in *Luther Today*, p.83.   142. Prenter, *op cit.*, pp. 110, 111.
143. Quoted in *Luther Today*, p.83.   144. H.E., III, p.349.
145. *ibid.* p.350.   146. Augustine, *De Doctrina*, II.
147. J.A. Quenstedt, *Theologia*, I, p.56.
148. *Bondage*, p.26.   149. W.A., XI, p.223.
150. M. Luther, *Römerbrief*, ed. J. Ficker, p.240.
151. W.A., III, p.643.   152. W.A., Tr. II, 439.
153. E.E., XLVI, p.338.   154. W.A., VIII, p.236.
155. H.E., II, p.432.   156. W.A., X, p.576.
157. H.E., VI, p.368.   158. *ibid.*, p.379.
159. *Römerbrief*, p.4.   160. Kramm, *op cit.*, p.114; H.E., VI, p.478.
161. E.C. Blackman, *Biblical Interpretation*, P.120.
162. H. Cunliffe-Jones, *The Authority of the Biblical Revelation*, p.102.
163. *Luther Today*, p.74.   164. W.A., III, p.515.
165. *ibid.*, pp. 403, 404; cf. Erich Roth, 'Martin Luther and the Continental Reformation' in Church *Quarterly Review*, CLIII, p.173.
166. *Luther Today*, p.84.
167. cf. Y. Brilioth, *Eucharistic Faith and Practice*, p.105; Seeberg, *op. cit.*, IV, pp. 382, 383.
168. Pieper, *op. cit.*, I, p.278.   169. St.L., IX, p.1238.
170. Grant, *op. cit.*, p.117.

EXPLANATORY NOTES

Communicatio idiomatum (p. 104) *The sharing of the distinctive features of the divine Christ with the human and vica versa.*

THE TRANSFERRED TRIUMPH
A Message for Eastertide
by Dr Skevington Wood

*'God be praised, he gives us the victory
through our Lord Jesus Christ'*

I Corinthians 15:57

We are accustomed to seeing the celebration of victory on the field of sport. The winners of the F.A. Cup Final do a lap of honour. A Wimbledon champion will jump the net. The referee will raise the arm of a successful boxer. A cricket team will come out on to the balcony to receive the applause of the crowd. These are all ways of signalizing a victory.

In this passage from 1 Corinthians 15 the apostle Paul is celebrating the greatest victory in history. It is more determinative than any battle ever fought or any war ever won. It is God's conquest in Christ over Satan, sin and death. It took place at the first Easter. And the exciting thing is this: it is a victory in which we may share, if we belong to Christ.

This lengthy chapter has to do with life after death, as the heading in the New English Bible informs us. Paul answers two questions raised by those in Corinth who had doubts about it all. Question One is in v.12: 'How can some of you say there is no resurrection of the dead?'. Is resurrection possible after the body has been disposed of in the grave? Paul explains that the difficulty really lies in the opposite direction, for resurrection presupposes such dissolution. Question Two is in v.35: 'How are the dead raised? In what kind of body?' It is in a body like that of the risen Lord Jesus - that is, one suitable to the spiritual condition of the new life after death as the resurrection body of Jesus was to the circumstances of *His* reappearance on earth.

But now a further and final question arises. What will happen to bring about this transformation when the Lord comes again? 'We shall all be changed', Paul tells us in v.51 - both those who have died (v.52) and those who will not die because they are still living on earth at the Return of Christ (v.51). And the essence of the change is that what is perishable will be clothed with what is imperishable and what is mortal must be clothed with immortality (v.53). When that has happened, then the saying of Scripture will come true: 'Death is swallowed up; victory is won!'

Two passages from the Old Testament seem to be in Paul's mind. One is Isaiah 25:7,8: 'On this mountain the Lord will swallow up the veil that shrouds all the people, the pall thrown over all the nations; he will swallow up death for ever.' The other is in Hosea 13:14. 'Shall I redeem him from Sheol? Shall I ransom him from death? Oh, for your plagues, O death! Oh, for your sting, Sheol!' Paul challenges death to provide the evidence of its alleged victory, now that Christ has conquered the tomb. 'O Death, where is your victory? O Death, where is your sting?' The answer is - Nowhere. Death has been deprived of its boasted victory, because Christ has extracted the sting of sin. No wonder the apostle can add: 'God be praised, he gives us the victory through our Lord Jesus Christ'. It is a transferred triumph. Christ's victory becomes ours through faith. 'The victory that defeats the world is our faith', writes John in 1 John 5:4, 'for who is victor over the world but he who believes that Jesus is the Son of God?'

Will you notice *three* things about this victory won by Christ for us through his death and resurrection?

1. **Victory is an accomplished fact.**
It is a fact of history. It has already been achieved at the Cross and the tomb. Karl Heim, the German theologian, declared that Christianity is based on 'the majesty of what has happened'. It appeals to events. At the outset of this chapter Paul explains that when he first visited Corinth as an evangelist he handed over to them 'the facts which had been imparted' to him (v.3). He was drawing on a very early tradition which may even go back to within a year or two of the crucifixion itself. And what are these facts? 'Christ died for our sins... he was buried... he was raised to life... he appeared.' This is not fiction: it is fact.

A distinguished New Testament scholar, Professor A. M. Hunter of Aberdeen, has gone on record as declaring that if he did not believe this fact he would never enter a pulpit again. 'Once in history one man left a gaping tomb in the wide graveyard of the world', he went on, 'and this victory is like the breach of a North Sea dyke, an event of apparently small importance, whose consequences are incalculable.'

Victory, then, is a fact. It is not something still to be gained. It has already been won. The decisive battle has been fought. The campaign will continue to the end of the age, but, as the hymn puts it, 'victory is secure'. It *is* secure, *now*. There is no shred of uncertainty. Satan is a defeated enemy. He will continue to skirmish, but God's ultimate triumph is assured. 'God be praised, he gives us the victory - now - through our Lord Jesus Christ.' It is an accomplished fact.

2. Victory is an enabling experience.

It is not simply something achieved by Christ. It is something he shares with us. He is the Conqueror and we too can be more than conquerors through the one who loves us. God gives us the victory and it is a present experience.

How does he enable us to participate in his victory? When Jesus rose from the dead, he did not resume the old life but passed into a different mode of being. He entered the world of the spirit. But did this mean that he had forsaken his followers? Had he left them as orphans? Not a bit of it! Indeed, that was just what he had promised not to do. 'I will not leave you bereft', he told them (John 14:18), 'I am coming back to you'. He is coming back in glory, of course, at the end of time, but he came back to them at Pentecost as a spiritual presence. He was with them and indeed took up his residence within.

In a striking observation, Principal James Denney once wrote that 'no apostle ever remembered Jesus'. They had no need to. He was still with them, unseen but not unknown. So his victory was an experience.

It may be for us. We can live a victorious Christian life because the Victor himself is alive and with us. Christ is our victory and as we know him as a living bright reality, we shall be enabled to conquer in the fight against sin now and death at the end.

Let me call in some testimonies from the past. Here is Samuel Rutherford imprisoned in Aberdeen for no other crime than fidelity to the gospel. 'Jesus Christ came to me in my cell last night', he wrote. Here is Dr R.W. Dale, the great Congregationalist preacher of Carr's Lane Chapel, Birmingham, in his study preparing an Easter message and crying 'Christ is alive, as alive as I am myself', as the reality of the risen Lord came on him 'like a burst of glory'. Here is Peter Taylor Forsyth confiding to us: 'I have had personal dealings with the risen Christ as my Saviour, nearer and dearer than my own flesh and blood'. Victory is an enabling experience.

3. Victory is a stimulating hope.

Although we can share the victory now, the consummation is at the end. We may be delivered from the fear of death right away, but one day we will be delivered from death itself. 'Because I live', said Jesus, 'you will live too'. Or, as Paul puts it, those who are 'in Christ' will eventually be 'with Christ' always.

In an age when hope is in short supply the Christian gospel promises a goal for the future not only here but hereafter. 'Where there's life there's hope' - so the familiar proverb runs. The converse is also true: 'Where there's hope there's life'. The hope of final victory over death and finding fulfilment in Christ for ever puts meaning and purpose into what so many today complain is a tedious and aimless existence. This added dimension is the answer to the prevailing cult of disillusioned nihilism - the conclusion that nothing matters any more.

Easter is the festival of hope. And hope in biblical terms is something more than the optimism of a Micawber who is always expecting something to turn up. It is based on the rock of reality and is not simply a matter of wish fulfilment or indulgence in fantasy. Easter is an event not a dream. The Easter faith stems from the Easter fact. Because Christ rose, we too will rise at last in him. Here is the hope that enables us to face death with calm acceptance.

In his autobiography, Dr Harry Whitley, who was minister of St Giles' Kirk, Edinburgh, tells of a memorable Easter during the Second World War. Serving as an army chaplain in Germany, he was taken desperately ill, after being wounded some months earlier and returning prematurely to the line. On Easter Day, 1945, he hung precariously between life and death. He received Communion from a fellow-chaplain, and then lay all morning quiet and wonderfully at peace. In one of those rare experiences of profound spiritual insight, he was made ready for whatever God had in store for him, whether it was to be in heaven or on earth. He knew that for him it was life either way.

Eventually, he recovered and after the War resumed his ministry in the Church of Scotland. On his first Easter Sunday at St Giles' it was all brought back to him as the choir sang some words of George Herbert for the anthem:

'Rise, heart: thy Lord is risen.
Sing his praise with delays,
Who takes thee by the hand,
That thou likewise with Him may'st rise.'

This is the Christian's inviolable hope. It is born at Easter. Since Christ has conquered death, so too may we.

Easter is more than a date on the calendar. It is meant to be part of our own experience. Christ's victory can be ours. Are we realizing it as we should? Let us praise God for the transferred triumph and seek to live it every day. Notice how Paul closes the chapter with an exhortation: 'Therefore, my beloved brothers, stand firm and immovable, and work for the Lord always, work without limit, since you know that in the Lord your labour cannot be lost'.

EPILOGUE

For some years Dr Wood had developed an interest in the life and ministry of William Grimshaw of Haworth (1708-63). He was invited by the Evangelical Library to give its Annual Lecture in 1963. His subject was William Grimshaw who died on 7th April, 1763. Dr Wood also preached the commemorative sermon at Haworth on the bi-centenary of Grimshaw's promotion to glory in the same year. During the course of the sermon he said that the secret of William Grimshaw's ministry was to be found on the sounding board of the pulpit at Haworth Church, Grimshaw's own pulpit. There, is inscribed 'For I determined not to know anything among you, save Jesus Christ, and him crucified' 1 Cor. 2 v2 (AV) and 'For me to live is Christ and to die is gain' Phil. 1 v21 (AV). These two verses formed the basis of Dr Wood's sermon at Haworth in 1963. They also formed the foundation of Dr Wood's own life and work. He never moved away from the central point of the gospel message, the Cross of Christ by which sinners are reconciled to God.

It seems fitting that this short tribute to the Revd Dr Arthur Skevington Wood should conclude with Charles Wesley's hymn, rarely sung today, which was composed on the death of the Revd William Grimshaw.

- 1 -

Thanks be to God, whose truth and power
And faithful mercies never end;
Who brings us through the mortal hour,
And bids our spotless soul ascend!

- 2 -

Thanks be to God, the God of love,
The giver of all-conquering grace,
Who calls our friend to joys above,
And shows him there His open face.

- 3 -

The God whom here his faith beheld,
The Father's fullness in the Son,
He sees, in glorious light reveal'd,
And shouts, and falls before the throne.

We, Saviour, at thy footstool lie,
We creatures purchased by Thy blood,
And 'Holy, holy, holy,' cry,
In honour of the triune God.

With angels and archangels join,
With all the ransom'd sons of grace,
Extol the majesty Divine,
And breathe unutterable praise.

We praise Thy constancy of love,
Which kept its favourite to the end;
Which soon shall all our souls remove,
Who trust in our eternal Friend.

To us who in Thy blood believe,
The world, the fiend, and sin tread down,
Thou wilt the final victory give,
And then the bright triumphant crown.

Charles Wesley.

This hymn was sung at the first meeting of the Wesley Fellowship following the death of Dr Wood to the tune 'Winchester New' (H & P 84).

APPENDIX I

This appendix is a catalogue of books written by Dr Arthur Skevington Wood. The dates given are those of first publications. Some books were republished in U.S.A. with changed titles; these are shown in brackets. The list is comprehensive but not necessarily exhaustive. It does not include the many booklets and pamphlets for which Dr Wood was also responsible.

Thomas Haweis	268 pp.	1957
And with Fire	176 pp.	1958 (Baptised with Fire)
The Inextinguishable Blaze	246 pp.	1960
Paul's Pentecost	144 pp.	1963 (Life in the Spirit)
Heralds of the Gospel	126 pp.	1963 (The Art of Preaching)
Prophecy in a Space Age	164 pp.	1964
Evangelism	119 pp.	1966
Principles of Biblical Interpretation	103 pp.	1967
The Burning Heart	286 pp.	1967
Captive to the Word	178 pp.	1969
Signs of the Times	126 pp.	1970
The Nature of Man	61 pp.	1972
For All Seasons	169 pp.	1979
What the Bible says about God	107 pp.	1980
The Call of God	68 pp.	1984
Revelation and Reason	92 pp.	1992

APPENDIX II

The following people have helped in various ways in the production of this book and gratitude to each is thus recorded.

Mr John Allen

Mr Peter Barker

Revd Howard A. G. Belben

Revd Norman Burrows

Mrs Alison Cartwright

Mr & Mrs A. Chester

Revd Dr William R. Davies

Mrs Avis Dawson

Mr David L. Gray

Mr Jack Henderson

Revd Alan J. Hughes

Revd John Job

Revd David Kingdon

Revd Gilbert Kirby

Mrs Gill Llewellyn

Professor I. Howard Marshall

Mr Jeremy Mudditt

Revd Dr Herbert McGonigle

Revd David G. Palmer

Revd Dr William Parkes

Mr Bill Parkinson

Mr Maurice Rowlandson

Mrs Margaret Taylor

Paisley Cliff Fellowship

We are particularly indebted to John Moorley and his staff for their invaluable advice and unfailing courtesy.

We are also grateful to Revd Howard Belben and Revd John Job for their willingness to read the final proofs.